Grow

Helping Others to Flourish
A Mentor's Guide
to the Early Career Framework

Katie Jump

ISBN: 9798665765341

Inspired by Fran, Nama and Natalie

CONTENTS

INTRODUCTION

This book is intended as a guide to mentors across the Primary Phase to help them get the most out of the opportunity to work with a Trainee Teacher, Newly Qualified Teacher or Early Career Teacher. Alongside information on the new framework, this book has ideas for supporting others at their stage of development; and reflecting on your own practice.

It is easy to see having a trainee teacher, or NQT, as an added burden to an already overflowing to-do list. But what about if you reframe it as an opportunity? A chance to share your expertise, your experience of making a million decisions all day every day (and the reasons behind them) to drive the learning of your class forward. You were chosen to be a mentor because of your skills, celebrate them! However, time is tight in schools, and you may not have had the chance to familiarise yourself with the new documentation. This book is designed as a step by step guide to working through the Early Career Framework in conjunction with the Teacher Standards giving ideas of activities for each level of mentee, but also has some ideas for mentors who want to take this chance to pause and reflect on their own practice. Each chapter includes a discussion based on the most up-to-date literature and research, so you can feel confident you are well informed to help your mentee.

At the end of each chapter there are tasks you might want to direct your mentee to complete to deepen their understanding of each of the Teachers' Standards.

These activities are divided into the following categories:

Review Literature	**Research**	**Discuss**	**Investigate**
Reflect	**Connect**	**View**	**Observe Colleagues**

The tasks are hierarchical in their level of complexity of thinking and understanding. You might choose to suggest a different level of task to that which is assigned to your mentee's position dependent on where you feel their strengths lie, or because you are aware of the time of year and other pressures on their workload.

It is important to remember the Early Career Framework is not designed as an assessment tool and should not be used as a box ticking mechanism. The inclusion of the Framework extracts in the following chapters are there as a reminder and to focus the discussion and subsequent direction of follow up work and ensure all areas are covered.

1 HIGH EXPECTATIONS

Overview

By the time you are at the point of reading this book, you will probably have taught thousands of lessons to hundreds of children; put up countless displays; set up several classrooms; and established class charters and table monitors on the 1st September many, many times. You have a preferred way of working; your children settle into your routines and the learning you planned takes place. It is actually quite tricky to pinpoint when you selected your way of doing things; how your approach to teaching evolved. Being able to unpick the sum parts of what makes your classroom work though, is exactly what your mentee needs you to be able to do. Whether you consciously realise it or not, your way of working will align with one or maybe aspects of several, educational theories. The discussion for this chapter aims to give you the opportunity to review key educational theories and consider where your approach to teaching sits. There is no 'right' or 'wrong' style to teach from, though hopefully you will be able to reflect on what is 'right' or 'wrong' for you. You may even be able to see links between techniques you prefer and larger educational theories that underpin your beliefs; and conversely why some techniques don't fit with your approach.

<table>
<tr><th colspan="2">Teachers' Standards</th></tr>
<tr><td colspan="2">A teacher must:
Set high expectations which inspire, motivate and challenge pupils<ul><li>establish a safe and stimulating environment for pupils, rooted in mutual respect</li><li>set goals that stretch and challenge pupils of all backgrounds, abilities and dispositions</li><li>demonstrate consistently the positive attitudes, values and behaviour which are expected of pupils.</li></ul></td></tr>
<tr><th colspan="2">Early Career Framework</th></tr>
<tr><td>Learn that...

1.Teachers have the ability to affect and improve the wellbeing, motivation and behaviour of their pupils.

2. Teachers are key role models, who can influence the attitudes, values and behaviours of their pupils.

3. Teacher expectations can affect pupil outcomes; setting goals that challenge and stretch pupils is essential.

4. Setting clear expectations can help communicate shared values that improve classroom and school culture.

5. A culture of mutual trust and respect supports effective relationships.</td><td>Learn how to...

Communicate a belief in the academic potential of all pupils, by:
• Using intentional and consistent language that promotes challenge and aspiration.
• Setting tasks that stretch pupils, but which are achievable, within a challenging curriculum.
• Creating a positive environment where making mistakes and learning from them and the need for effort and perseverance are part of the daily routine.
• Seeking opportunities to engage parents and carers in the education of their children (e.g. proactively highlighting successes).

Demonstrate consistently high</td></tr>
</table>

6. High-quality teaching has a long-term positive effect on pupils' life chances, particularly for children from disadvantaged backgrounds	behavioural expectations, by: • Creating a culture of respect and trust in the classroom that supports all pupils to succeed (e.g. by modelling the types of courteous behaviour expected of pupils). • Teaching and rigorously maintaining clear behavioural expectations (e.g. for contributions, volume level and concentration). • Applying rules, sanctions and rewards in line with school policy, escalating behaviour incidents as appropriate. • Acknowledging and praising pupil effort and emphasising progress being made.

Discussion

You won't necessarily be able to immediately say whether you are a behaviourist or constructivist in your approach to teaching, however our education system has evolved through the influences of both perspectives and their legacy is visible in most schools today. The following paragraphs set out the key educational aspects of each of these terms, and the actions which may be seen in school that are influenced by them. As you read each paragraph, consider which ideas are promoted in your school, which you believe makes for a great teaching environment and which -if any- make you shudder.

Behaviourism is a broad psychological term which encompasses the work of Pavlov, Watson, Thorndike and Skinner amongst others. The work of B.F. Skinner though, can be seen to inform a particular perspective on education specifically. The behaviourist's view of the purpose of education is based on the notion that humans can be conditioned to act based upon consequences. By rewarding learners for 'good' behaviour (mainly through praise and reward), they can be conditioned to seek out this reward repeatedly and will learn the behaviours which will make this happen. In school, working hard, completing tasks and following school rules are all examples of behaviourism. Whilst Skinner encouraged what he termed operant conditioning to reinforce positive behaviour, he did not feel the counterbalance of punishment was as effective. The reasons for this were two-fold. Firstly, because tests on animals (this was the 1930s!) had not shown as strong a correlation between displaying a lack of desired behaviour and punishment as the opposite. Secondly, he raised the suggestion that those displaying negative behaviour and receiving the interaction that punishment involved may actually be rewarded, if it is the social interaction itself that was being perceiving as reward. If you have seen a similar reaction in a child in your class and altered the way you react accordingly, you have applied this theory to your practice.

Skinner's behaviouristic view of reward reinforcing behaviour extends beyond behaviour management to teaching. Behaviourists would argue that all children being expected to work at the same pace and on the same task would not be making a connection between effort and the reward of tasks that reflect their ability. Similarly, extended periods between tasks being completed and feedback being received would also dilute the operant conditioning effect.

When knowledge itself is viewed through a behaviourist lens, it is seen as a true reflection of the world, and that teachers hold the knowledge and choose how and when to impart it to the learner. Competition is used to encourage the acquisition of knowledge, and learners are the receivers of knowledge that already exists, rather than participating in any co-creation (Murphy in Twining et al, 2017).

There are three sub-sections of a Constructivist approach: Cognitive, Radical and Social. Whilst they all believe learners to be active creators of knowledge through their interactions with the world and others, and that learning is built upon prior knowledge and experience; it is their views on the role of the teacher that make them distinct from each other. Cognitive constructivists perceive teachers as a guide to learners through experiences which they have predetermined, and whilst no two learners experience the exact same thing, there is an intended sequence that is planned for learners to actively participate in. The idea that knowledge is explicit but is also built upon by experience and then abstraction can be seen currently in classrooms through the use of the concrete, pictorial, abstract methods in mathematics. Jean Piaget's theory of cognitive development suggested children move through four stages of development, which can be broadly seen through this CPA approach. The first, sensorimotor, is when children begin to understand the permanence of objects; the second, preoperational, is when children can think using symbols as they know enough about the real world to transfer this knowledge into pictorial representation. His third stage, concrete operational, is a period when children could think with more complexity and begin to problem solve, though support through physical or pictorial representation would be needed. Formal operational, the final stage, was believed by Piaget as something achieved between 12 and 19 and was the ability to solve hypothetical dilemmas. This has been translated into what we commonly now see in maths lessons as children move through the use of concrete, pictorial and abstract activities as they engage with mathematical concepts. If you are confident in using this approach and can see its benefits, your practice is aligned with Cognitive constructivism.

Radical constructivists also perceive learning to take place through experience, but the dissonance between what is already understood and how a new piece of knowledge fits with this is where the learning is seen to take place. The role of the teacher then, is to find out what children already know and then construct learning to build upon this. The learning sequence may be less prescribed and whilst the teacher is heavily involved cognitively in decisions about next steps, the learner may feel more in control of the direction.

Social constructivists, like Vygotsky, view learning as mainly taking place within the dialogue with others, and as such, a social constructivist teacher would be an active participant in conversations about knowledge. A belief that social, cultural and historical influences play a huge role in constructing knowledge would inform their teaching. Their role would be to scaffold the learner, and the process of learning would be more of a focus than the knowledge itself. If you are competent practitioner of dialogic talk, then possibly you align most closely with this theory. Vygotsky also developed the term 'Zone of Proximal Development', or ZPD, which can be described as the fine edge between what is already known and where the new learning takes place. Designing lessons that are precisely balanced at this point for all pupils is no mean feat but can be helped by the culture of learners being intrinsically motivated that a social constructivist teacher would have developed in their classroom. Jerome Bruner built upon Vygotsky's ideas of ZPD, encouraging the use of a spiral curriculum to continually build upon prior learning. He also promoted the social aspect of creating knowledge and did not value the use of rote learning to retain knowledge.

Beyond these overarching ideas about the purpose of education, the climate of the classroom is also influenced by the attitudes held about how to learn successfully. Adopting meta-cognition strategies, or thinking about thinking (e.g. planning, persevering, making links, capitalising on resources or reasoning) can make learning both more efficient and effective. Claxton's (2002) concept of building learning power extols an attitude that it doesn't matter if learning is hard, if you have the ability to persevere and demonstrate resilience; it doesn't matter if learning is complex if we have the skills to question and reason. Meta-cognition is a level above the decisions about how best to obtain or deliver knowledge; it is about developing your pupils into learners who see themselves as having a learner identity, who have the skillset to engage with every learning opportunity.

Being a successful learner in recent years has become synonymous with the need to have a 'growth mindset' (Dweck, 2013) and classrooms adorned with 'I can't do it...yet!' can be found up and down the country. However, Dweck herself notes that in some cases her original work has been so distilled from its true meaning it can have little or no effect. She updated her book in 2017 to reflect this need to address the misconception. The notion of 'praising the effort that it takes to make progress or achieve' had become 'praise the effort' and so the impact was lost as children could see through the veil of praise when they themselves could see that very little had been achieved. The core principle of having a growth mindset is that becoming successful takes effort, not everything will come easily but that doesn't mean we don't try. Personally, I prefer Henry Ford's adage 'whether you think you can, or you think you can't, you're usually right'. The fine line a teacher needs to tread is knowing when there has been effort and when something has come easily, when very little appears to have been achieved but the effort and progress has been tremendous and to praise accordingly. The advantage a primary school teacher has over a secondary colleague is the time they are given to get to know the individuals in their class over the year. This is of enormous benefit to aiding these decisions, as giving praise is far more nuanced than it may seem at first. A classroom where praise is liberally handed out for anything and everything is a no more conducive learning environment than one where no praise is given at all. Children are shrewder than we give them credit for, they know genuine comments when they hear them.

Another way in which Dweck's mindset theories have been corrupted is the notion that everyone can be equally successful. Perseverance and determination will help us all improve to some extent, indeed there was once a belief that 10,000 hours practice would make you proficient in anything. Whilst this has been modified by the acknowledgement it is intelligent practice (modifying what you are doing based on results) that is far more productive, as a general rule the more you do something the better you get. We also need to acknowledge some people will display a flair or innate ability to do some things- they are our geniuses, our leaders in their field. In the classroom, we have to maintain a balance between praising the effort that it has taken to do something, whilst also recognising that sometimes work is enormously impressive, although it was not that difficult to achieve for a talented child. We need to acknowledge that not praising children for incredible things simply because it came easily to them may feel like it is in keeping with praising the effort but is no way to build relationships. It can lead to a reversed hierarchy to that which has been perceived historically (i.e. the 'high achievers' always get rewarded becomes the children who struggle are praised for achieving little), but it is a hierarchy, nonetheless. Maintaining the mutual respect and positive environment is far more complex than setting up reward systems and sticking to them regardless.

Learning Activities

Supporting Trainee Teachers

Look at the school prospectus (either online or a physical copy). What messages does it give about the school? Take a learning walk around the building and make notes on the attitudes and values you can see in the people and objects around the site. Observe a break time and investigate how children play together. How do your findings from these different activities correlate? Are you able to get a 'feel' for the setting and its aspirations?

Supporting Newly Qualified Teachers

Read Chapter One of 'Walkthrus' by Tom Sherrington and Oliver Caviglioli (2020). This chapter outlines some fundamentals of establishing the culture and expectations in your classroom. The rest of the book also covers many more of the areas of the teacher standards and is well worth reading.

Supporting Early Career Teachers

It is never too late to learn by observing another teacher! Think of the teachers in your school who have classroom environments or a classroom culture you seek to emulate and ask to observe them. As well as observing teaching techniques, make a conscious decision to observe how the children work within the routines and layout of the classroom and evaluate whether there are any strategies that would work for you.

Growing as a Mentor

Read 'Understanding and Using Educational Theories' (Aubrey and Riley, 2019). Each chapter summarises a key educationalist, so you may want to research those you are less familiar with. Can you align the vision you have for your classroom (and your opinions on how best to educate) with any one theorist or movement? Being able to articulate this is difficult, but once you can, it sheds light on why you prefer certain techniques and teaching styles.

References

Aubrey, K. Riley, A. (2019) Understanding and Using Educational Theories, SAGE, London

Claxton, G. (2002) Building Learning Power, TLO, Bristol

Dweck, C. (2013) Mindset: New Psychology of Success, Random House, New York

Dweck, C. (2017) Updated Edition: Changing the way you think to fulfil your potential, Random House, New York

Sherrington, T. Caviglioli. O. (2020) Walkthrus, John Catt Educational, Woodbridge

Twining, P. Browne, N. Murphy, P. Hempel-Jorgensen, A. Harrison, S. & Parmar, N. (2017). New Purposes, New Practices, New Pedagogy Meta-Analysis, Researchgate, available at https://www.researchgate.net/publication/319711002_NP3_New_Purposes_New_Practices_New_Pedagogy_Meta-analysis_Report

Vygotsky, L. (1978) Mind in Society, Harvard University Press, Cambridge

2 HOW PUPILS LEARN

Overview

Thankfully, most schools have moved away from an expectation that a teacher's own performance should be measured solely from a set of data generated by pupil outcomes. However, as a professional community it is inherent in us to want to do the best for the children in our care, to want to teach them in a way that information 'sticks' and that they are able to build on this knowledge and be able to select the precise information they need to apply in different contexts. There is a tremendous amount of teacher led research now available, and it is more accessible than ever through twitter, blogs, TEDTalks and professional bodies such as the Chartered College. Whilst following every piece of research blindly will do us no favours, being well informed of the current thinking on how best to teach effectively and again making conscious decisions as to how - or whether - to apply it to our own practice is a skill that should be made explicit when modelling for less experienced teachers.

<table>
<tr><th colspan="2">Teachers' Standards</th></tr>
<tr><td colspan="2">A teacher must:
Promote good progress and outcomes by pupils
• be accountable for pupils' attainment, progress and outcomes
• be aware of pupils' capabilities and their prior knowledge, and plan teaching to build on these
• guide pupils to reflect on the progress they have made and their emerging needs
• demonstrate knowledge and understanding of how pupils learn and how this impacts on teaching
• encourage pupils to take a responsible and conscientious attitude to their own work and study.</td></tr>
<tr><th colspan="2">Early Career Framework</th></tr>
<tr><td>Learn that...

1. Learning involves a lasting change in pupils' capabilities or understanding.

2. Prior knowledge plays an important role in how pupils learn; committing some key facts to their long-term memory is likely to help pupils learn more complex ideas.

3. An important factor in learning is memory, which can be thought of as comprising two elements: working memory and long-term memory.

4. Working memory is where information that is being actively</td><td>Learn how to...

Avoid overloading working memory, by:
• Taking into account pupils' prior knowledge when planning how much new information to introduce.
• Breaking complex material into smaller steps (e.g. using partially completed examples to focus pupils on the specific steps).
• Reducing distractions that take attention away from what is being taught (e.g. keeping the complexity of a task to a minimum, so that attention is focused on the content).</td></tr>
</table>

processed is held, but its capacity is limited and can be overloaded. 5. Long-term memory can be considered as a store of knowledge that changes as pupils learn by integrating new ideas with existing knowledge. 6. Where prior knowledge is weak, pupils are more likely to develop misconceptions, particularly if new ideas are introduced too quickly. 7. Regular purposeful practice of what has previously been taught can help consolidate material and help pupils remember what they have learned. 8. Requiring pupils to retrieve information from memory, and spacing practice so that pupils revisit ideas after a gap are also likely to strengthen recall. 9. Worked examples that take pupils through each step of a new process are also likely to support pupils to learn.	Build on pupils' prior knowledge, by: • Identifying possible misconceptions and planning how to prevent these forming. • Linking what pupils already know to what is being taught (e.g. explaining how new content builds on what is already known). • Sequencing lessons so that pupils secure foundational knowledge before encountering more complex content. • Encouraging pupils to share emerging understanding and points of confusion so that misconceptions can be addressed. Increase likelihood of material being retained, by: • Balancing exposition, repetition, practice and retrieval of critical knowledge and skills. • Planning regular review and practice of key ideas and concepts over time. • Designing practice, generation and retrieval tasks that provide just enough support so that pupils experience a high success rate when attempting challenging work. • Increasing challenge with

	practice and retrieval as knowledge becomes more secure (e.g. by removing scaffolding, lengthening spacing or introducing interacting elements).

Discussion

There are three main categories of memory: sensory, short term and long term. Sensory memory is the most fleeting as our brains do not always encode what we have noticed through our senses. Long term memory can be further categorised into procedural (learned skills), episodic (experiences and events - often recent and mundane e.g. whether you bought milk yesterday), semantic (facts and knowledge), and autobiographical (significant personal events). The most crucial category for day-to-day teaching is our short-term, working memory.

Children with poor working memory can be seen to make slower academic progress; be reserved when working in groups; have difficulties in following instructions; have noticeable problems when activities involve processing and storage, appear to have a short attention span and be distracted easily. When working independently they can also have place-keeping difficulties. (Gathercole and Homes, 2014). The important point after identifying this in a pupil is acting upon what the research suggests will mitigate these issues in the classroom context. Reducing the amount of information that needs to be stored to complete a task; repeating instructions and providing visual reminders; using memory aids such as mnemonics; playing memory games to develop strategies and reducing the difficulty of what is to be processed into smaller steps will all assist a pupil with working memory issues (Katz, 2011).

One of the ways to access more working memory capacity is through the use of dual coding. By providing information through two channels (visual and verbal), Paivio (1990) explains a connection is made between them in our brains. This enables the brain to encode the information in our working memory into our long-term memory. Having both visual and verbal information about the same concept makes it easier for the brain to retrieve this information when it needs to be recalled at a later date. It can be used in many ways in the classroom: through the use of visual representations in maths; carefully selecting images to accompany oral explanations; and with older pupils, teaching them how to design notes about what they are learning with accompanying icons. However, it is not as simple as just presenting pictures alongside teacher explanations, and time and consideration is needed to ensure the connections between the two information streams are optimal. The work of Oliver Caviglioli (2019) on this topic provides clear techniques underpinned by research in this area.

John Sweller's (1990) paper on Cognitive Load Theory asserts that it is necessary for a learner to have a strong basis of knowledge in their long-term memory on a given topic before they are asked to problem solve. He explains it is ineffectual to ask children to problem solve without a strong schema of knowledge about a topic. Kirschner (2020) summarises Sweller's ideas when he explains that without having a strong knowledge base from which to select relevant information and strategies that have worked in the past, learners tend to use means-ends analysis. A means-ends analysis is the process of looking at where you need to be (in this case the solution) and your current position. You would then continually reflect on how close your actions have taken you to where you need to be and adapting your actions accordingly. In school, this is similar to a poor trial and error activity which we may see in maths lessons when children are unable to work systematically as their information field for what they have to do is too large, or they are expected to work out a solution without the necessary mathematical knowledge to complete the task. The implication of this is that a preoccupation with current position and how near/far it is to the end goal takes a significant amount of working memory space. The working memory is preoccupied with searching for the information needed to solve a problem, whereas a child who is knowledgeable about a topic can analyse the knowledge they have and select the aspects that are most appropriate to solve the problem in hand. Sweller also notes that whilst superficially it may look as if learning has taken place because the task has been completed, long-term memory has not been altered by the acquisition of new knowledge. We have to then ask ourselves as teachers what have we actually accomplished beyond keeping children busy for an hour? He concludes by suggesting five implications which teachers must take into consideration: there is a heavy cognitive load on learners if they have to problem solve before becoming knowledgeable about a topic; the skills to solve problems and to make connections between pieces of knowledge are very different; the effort of problem solving inhibits the acquisition of knowledge; without the knowledge needed, it is difficult to develop problem solving expertise; and that simply practising problem solving doesn't necessarily improve problem solving skills.

Ensuring that knowledge is acquired and secured in long-term memory is fundamentally what it means to be a teacher. The Early Career Framework makes specific reference to many of the techniques identified by Barack Rosenshine in his 2012 article on the principles of direct instruction. There are ten principles which have been proven as highly effective through research into cognitive science, analysing the work of master teachers and investigating that which acts as a cognitive support.

The principles are:
1) Perform a daily review of previous learning
2) Introduce new material in small steps to support working memory
3)Ask questions of all learners to check understanding
4) Provide models and think aloud
5) Guide practice and use many examples

6)Frequently check understanding
7)Ensure a high success rate for pupils (about 80%) to optimise pupil engagement
8)Use temporary supports and scaffolds for difficult tasks
9)Provide opportunities for independent practice as overlearning is important to retain knowledge
10) Review what has been learned regularly by returning to it weekly and monthly to build the connections necessary.

The skill of the experienced teacher is to know when to apply these techniques and which ones are most appropriate for the knowledge that needs to be passed on. Combined with an understanding of how to optimise the working memory through careful presentation of information and informed task choice, we are at a point where research has given us insight into the most efficient and proficient ways to help pupils learn.

Learning Activities

Supporting Trainee Teachers

Watch this talk by Peter Doolittle for a brief introduction to working memory. Can you think of examples where your working memory has become overloaded? https://www.ted.com/talks/peter_doolittle_how_your_working_memory_makes_sense_of_the_world?language=en Schools use a WMRS assessment to identify working memory issues. Ask the SENDCo in your setting to show you how a WMRS test works.

Supporting Newly Qualified Teachers

Listen to the Education Endowment Foundation Podcast 'Trialled and Tested' episode about the importance of considering working memory.
https://evidencebased.education/working-memory/

Supporting Early Career Teachers

Read the Chartered College article written by Shibli and West about Cognitive Load Theory. There are many further readings at the end of the article if this is an area you would like to learn more about. https://impact.chartered.college/article/shibli-cognitive-load-theory-classroom/

Growing as a Mentor

Watch John Sweller's presentation on Cognitive Load Theory from the ACE conference/ ResearchED, Melbourne (2017)
https://www.youtube.com/watchtime_continue=7&v=gOLPfi9Ls-w&feature=emb_logo

For a broader understanding of all aspects of learning and the associated psychology, read 'How Learning Happens' (Kirschner and Hendrick, 2020)

References

Caviglioli, O. (2010), Dual Coding with Teachers, John Catt Education, Woodbridge

Gathercole, S. Holmes, G. (2014) Supporting Children with working memory problems presentation and workshop, MRC Cognition and Brain Science Unit

Katz, M. (2011) *Classroom Strategies for improving working memory* in CHADD, February 2011 edition

Kirschner, P. Hendrick, C. (2020) How Learning Happens, Routledge, Oxford

Paivio, A. (1990) Mental Representations, A Dual Coding Approach, Oxford Science, Oxford

Rosenshine, B. (2012) *Principles of instruction: research-based strategies that all teachers should know,* in American Educator, American Federation of Teachers, AFL-CIO, 36(1), p12.

Sweller, J. (1988) *Cognitive Load During Problem Solving: Effects on Learning* in Cognitive Science (12), pp257-285

3 CURRICULUM

Overview

Opinions on what constitutes a good curriculum are so numerous it would be impossible to distil them into one book chapter. The same could be said of the evolutions and forms the curriculum has undergone since its introduction in 1988. This chapter contains a brief understanding of where the current curriculum has evolved from, and the political influences on it, which may help you explain the thoughts behind the current practice your mentee will see in school. Whilst the direction the entire curriculum of your school is heading may not be your decision, the comprehensive understanding you have of the subject(s) you lead is something to share with your mentee. Where your subject 'sits' within the curriculum vision, as well as what your year group adds to the learning journey of children in your school will help your mentee understand the complexities of constructing a balanced curriculum that does its best for pupils. The knowledge vs problem-solving debate was explored in the previous chapter, here we will look at knowledge vs discovery in the context of a subject leader and mentor.

<table>
<tr><th colspan="2">Teachers' Standards</th></tr>
<tr><td colspan="2">A teacher must:
Demonstrate good subject and curriculum knowledge
• have a secure knowledge of the relevant subject(s) and curriculum areas, foster and maintain pupils' interest in the subject, and address misunderstandings
• demonstrate a critical understanding of developments in the subject and curriculum areas, and promote the value of scholarship
• demonstrate an understanding of and take responsibility for promoting high standards of literacy, articulacy and the correct use of standard English, whatever the teacher's specialist subject
• if teaching early reading, demonstrate a clear understanding of systematic synthetic phonics
• if teaching early mathematics, demonstrate a clear understanding of appropriate teaching strategies.</td></tr>
<tr><th colspan="2">Early Career Framework</th></tr>
<tr><td>Learn that...

1. A school's curriculum enables it to set out its vision for the knowledge, skills and values that its pupils will learn, encompassing the national curriculum within a coherent wider vision for successful learning.

2. Secure subject knowledge helps teachers to motivate pupils and teach effectively.</td><td>Learn how to...

Deliver a carefully sequenced and coherent curriculum, by:
• Identifying essential concepts, knowledge, skills and principles of the subject and providing opportunity for all pupils to learn and master these critical components.
• Ensuring pupils' thinking is focused on key ideas within the subject.</td></tr>
</table>

3. Ensuring pupils master foundational concepts and knowledge before moving on is likely to build pupils' confidence and help them succeed. 4. Anticipating common misconceptions within particular subjects is also an important aspect of curricular knowledge; working closely with colleagues to develop an understanding of likely misconceptions is valuable. 5. Explicitly teaching pupils the knowledge and skills they need to succeed within particular subject areas is beneficial. 6. In order for pupils to think critically, they must have a secure understanding of knowledge within the subject area they are being asked to think critically about. 7. In all subject areas, pupils learn new ideas by linking those ideas to existing knowledge, organising this knowledge into increasingly complex mental models (or "schemata"); carefully sequencing teaching to facilitate this process is important. 8. Pupils are likely to struggle to	• Working with experienced colleagues to accumulate and refine a collection of powerful analogies, illustrations, examples, explanations and demonstrations. • Using resources and materials aligned with the school curriculum (e.g. textbooks or shared resources designed by experienced colleagues that carefully sequence content). • Being aware of common misconceptions and discussing with experienced colleagues how to help pupils master important concepts. Support pupils to build increasingly complex mental models, by: • Discussing curriculum design with experienced colleagues and balancing exposition, repetition, practice of critical skills and knowledge. • Revisiting the big ideas of the subject over time and teaching key concepts through a range of examples. • Drawing explicit links between new content and the core concepts and principles in the subject

transfer what has been learnt in one discipline to a new or unfamiliar context. 9. To access the curriculum, early literacy provides fundamental knowledge; reading comprises two elements: word reading and language comprehension; systematic synthetic phonics is the most effective approach for teaching pupils to decode. 10. Every teacher can improve pupils' literacy, including by explicitly teaching reading, writing and oral language skills specific to individual disciplines.	Develop fluency, by: • Providing tasks that support pupils to learn key ideas securely (e.g. quizzing pupils so they develop fluency with times tables). • Using retrieval and spaced practice to build automatic recall of key knowledge. Help pupils apply knowledge and skills to other contexts, by: • Ensuring pupils have relevant domain-specific knowledge, especially when being asked to think critically within a subject. • Interleaving concrete and abstract examples, slowly withdrawing concrete examples and drawing attention to the underlying structure of problems. Develop pupils' literacy, by: • Demonstrating a clear understanding of systematic synthetic phonics, particularly if teaching early reading and spelling. • Supporting younger pupils to become fluent readers and to write fluently and legibly. • Teaching unfamiliar vocabulary explicitly and planning for pupils

	to be repeatedly exposed to high-utility and high-frequency vocabulary in what is taught. • Modelling reading comprehension by asking questions, making predictions, and summarising when reading. • Promoting reading for pleasure (e.g. by using a range of whole class reading approaches and regularly reading high-quality texts to children). • Modelling and requiring high-quality oral language, recognising that spoken language underpins the development of reading and writing (e.g. requiring pupils to respond to questions in full sentences, making use of relevant technical vocabulary). • Teaching different forms of writing by modelling planning, drafting and editing.

Discussion

The National Curriculum, as we know it today was introduced by Kenneth Baker in 1988. Concern had been building for years that the education system (which had been largely untouched since the war) and was run at a devolved level by local authorities, was not conducive to the high standards of education desired for the country. Alongside changes to how pupils gained spaces in schools and performance criteria, the Education Reform Act established the need for a national curriculum. Three core subjects and seven foundation subjects were included, and subject content for each was introduced. The benefit of this was that children could move schools and not be disadvantaged transferring between different curriculums. It was also part of this overhaul that Standard Attainment Tests (or SATs) were introduced for 7, 11 and 14-year-olds. The political driver for this change was the intention to make education a consumer led concept, affording parents information and choice about different schools.

Teachers felt the quantity of this new curriculum was unwieldy, and in 1993, Sir Ron Dearing carried out a review which led to a revised edition (published in 1995) with a decrease in the quantity of specified content.

In 1997, Labour came to power and the then Secretary of State, David Blunkett, ordered another review. His main concern about the curriculum as it stood was that not enough time was given to the basics of becoming numerate and literate, and so in the 1999 version, which came into force in 2000, the statutory requirement of an hour of English and Maths per day was introduced. The requirements for these two subjects (the Literacy and Numeracy hours as they were then titled) were in much more detail, drilling down into what should be taught in every block, which was further sub-divided into weekly and daily tasks. If you haven't seen these strategies, or their next incarnation in 2006, I suggest you follow the links in the references to see the level of detail prescribed. The 2006 versions of both strategies stepped back slightly with their level of detail, with the intention of giving teachers and schools more autonomy on how to group objectives and plan units. As someone who worked through this period and had mentoring responsibilities for NQTs, it was evident at the time that the main drawback was that newer teachers who had not gained the knowledge that came with using the 1999 frameworks, and had to start with the 2006 versions, actually found it more difficult as the level of detailed subject knowledge given in the previous version was missing.

Alongside a tightening of core subjects at this time, the Qualifications and Curriculum Authority (QCA) produced schemes of work for every foundation subject area. Subjects had between 3 and 6 of these planning documents for individual topics which covered the entire curriculum content expected. Teachers were able to use these as a framework to base their planning around, and you may even see topics like the Design and Technology 'Fairgrounds' Y6 topic, or 'Moving Vehicles' Y2 topic still in some guise in subject plans today. Again, if you do have not seen these documents, follow the link in the references to an example. The DT Association has continued in this vein and has designed documents called 'Projects on a page' which can be used in a similar way.

In 2007, the government commissioned Sir Jim Rose to review the curriculum and he came up with 25 recommendations. One of the most well-known was the changes to phonics teaching towards a synthetic phonics approach. Regarding core subjects, Rose suggested that Maths, English and ICT should be considered core, and that KS2 should include the teaching of a Modern Foreign Language. He also noted that rather than being triggered in a reactionary way, reviews of the National Curriculum across all phases should be timetabled for regular review.

When the Conservative government came back into power in 2010, it changed the title of the Department for Education to the Department for Children, Schools and Families and abolished the Qualifications and Standards Authority. In 2011, they announced a review of the national curriculum. This curriculum came into force in 2014. Some of the main criticisms of this curriculum were that foundation subjects seemed to be marginalised as the statutory content was sparse in comparison to the core subjects, there were no statutory requirements for speaking and listening, and that PSHE and Citizenship had been removed as a statutory subject altogether. The government were keen to state that this change in curriculum was to ensure that England matched the standards of other countries in its outcomes for pupils, and the expectations for the end of Key Stage 2 are certainly dramatically increased in comparison to the previous curriculum. The debate as to how achievable this is for all children though, continues. Most schools continue to assign one hour a day to English and Maths teaching as they introduced in the 1990s, many would say it is more of a struggle than ever to cover the quantity of foundation learning that they aspire to.

Much has been made of the term adopted by Ofsted in 2019 of a 'broad and balanced curriculum' in its inspection framework. However, throughout all the documents mentioned previously, the term broad and balanced has appeared repeatedly since the Education Reform Act of 1988. Whilst it is not new, including it in the inspection framework is a reaction to noticing that schools have felt compelled to narrow their curriculum offer to ensure the high standards expected in English and Maths are met. So, this may be considered the heyday for subject leaders of foundation subjects, no? The answer varies enormously dependent on the school you work in, unfortunately. If your school has always taken the approach of providing a broad and balanced curriculum, then this may be a time for tweaking your current planning and being allocated more curriculum time to your subject. If you have had to make way for Maths and English teaching for years, your subject may be in a poor position. Three new buzzwords, intent, impact and implementation have left subject leaders in some schools in the position of drafting up summaries to crystallise the position of their subject. The decisions about what each subject provides, though, need to be viewed from the wider perspective of the curriculum as a whole. In a piece I wrote for Impact magazine (2019), I discussed the role of art as a subject and how it can be planned dependent on what the school's approach to curriculum is. Based on the work of Eisner, who discusses the eight visions that could underpin art teaching, I would suggest any subject leader could look to the positions he outlines and decide what they wish their subject to offer the curriculum of their school.

Thinking back to your educational stance in Chapter 1, you may have a very strong opinion on the knowledge vs discovery debate. Whether you believe transmitting knowledge is the key to your subject, or that it is the pupils who should construct and discover the knowledge through the experiences provided, may underpin what you believe effective teaching to be. Maybe you believe different subjects should be at different points on this continuum, or that the start of a topic belongs firmly in the knowledge camp, and the end of a topic should be more about discovery (or the problem-solving discussed in Chapter 2). This is known in educational fields as the traditionalist vs progressive debate. John Dewey (1938) explains these two standpoints and what they mean in relation to your view on what constitutes good teaching. The challenge- and it does seem to be more of an issue in primary school due to how observations and performance management are carried out- is if your opinion on teaching (both in and out of your subject) does not align with the values of your school. Hopefully, the push for clarity on intent, impact and implementation by Ofsted will make it easier for teachers to ask these questions when looking at new schools and judge for themselves if they agree with the beliefs of the school. Whether you consider yourself traditionalist or progressive, it's important to be able to be able to verbalise and explain your opinion based on your own experience; and of course the important aspect of being a mentor is being able to articulate this and the reasons behind your thinking.

Learning Activities

Supporting Trainee Teachers

Discuss with your mentor the previous year groups they have worked in. Listen to what they notice about how strands of curriculum develop over the primary phase. What subjects are divided into content for each key stage, what subjects are further divided by lower and upper phase? Which subjects have year group specific content? Which revisit key ideas every year?

Supporting Newly Qualified Teachers

In your NQT time, take the opportunity to observe a foundation subject in the year below and above the one you are teaching in. If possible, make it a subject you have already taught as part of your timetable. How does the curriculum in your year group fit into the bigger picture? What aspects of the previous year group do you rely on children knowing really well? Is there anything you assumed they didn't know but have now found out has already been covered?

Supporting Early Career Teachers

Choose a foundation subject in your school (science is a really good example) and look at the planning for each age phase (Key Stage One, Lower and Upper Key Stage Two). Select a scientific area, for example 'Animals, including Humans'. Can you track the foundations of learning in Key Stage One and how these are built upon in each phase? Do you refer to key concepts from previous years when you are teaching the subject to your class? Look ahead to the year group above you- what are they teaching and how is it supported by your work the previous year?

Growing as a Mentor

Twitter has a huge educator community. Try following @ClareSealy for more information on a spiral curriculum; @MrBoothY6 for planning; @SchoolsWeek for updates on education policy; @WhiteRoseMaths for maths resources and training, @ImpactWales for visual representations of key learning principles and @CharteredColl for research carried out and presented by teachers. You could also follow your local SCITT or university account for mentoring CPD.

References

Dearing, R. 1993 The National Curriculum and its Assessment: Final Report, School Curriculum & Assessment Authority, London available at http://www.educationengland.org.uk/documents/dearing1994/dearing1994.html

Department for Education (1988) Education Reform Act 1988, http://www.educationengland.org.uk/documents/acts/1988-education-reform-act.pdf

Department for Education, (1999) National Numeracy Strategy – extract from Year 4, Unit 2 Addition and Subtraction https://www.middlesbrough.gov.uk/sites/default/files/Y4%20unit%202%20spring%20Addition%20and%20subtraction.pdf

Department for Education (2006) Primary framework for literacy and mathematics http://www.educationengland.org.uk/documents/pdfs/2006-primary-national-strategy.pdf

Design and Technology Association, (first published 2013, updated 2019) Projects on a page https://www.data.org.uk/shop-products/projects-on-a-page-sample/

Dewey, J. (1938) Experience and Education, Kappa Delta Pi. New York

Eisner, E. (2002) The Arts and Creation of Mind, Yale University Press, New Haven

Jump, K. (2019) *Principles and Techniques that underpin art teaching* in Impact, Journal of the Chartered College, Issue 7, available at https://impact.chartered.college/article/principles-and-techniques-underpin-art-teaching/

Qualifications and Curriculum Authority (1998) Design and Technology Unit 1A Mechanisms available at https://webarchive.nationalarchives.gov.uk/20100512173138/http://www.standards.dfes.gov.uk/pdf/primaryschemes/det1a.pdf

Rose, J (2008) Independent Review of the Primary Curriculum Final Report, DCSF publications, Nottingham available at https://dera.ioe.ac.uk/30098/2/2009-IRPC-final-report_Redacted.pdf

4 CLASSROOM PRACTICE

Overview

When I think of my own teaching on a busy day, I am often reminded of a conductor leading an orchestra. There are routine tasks that are performed every day, and like clockwork the schedule of registers, breaktimes, assemblies and home times are met like an underlying rhythm. When you are running late or have time to spare, you ensure the tempo speeds up or slows down accordingly. On top of this you are asking the majority to complete one task whilst keeping alert to the outliers who have a different job to complete. Timing one group to finish at the exact moment you have time to discuss their learning, before moving on to the next group. As well as all this, listening carefully to the entire group and sensing when the pitch or activity needs to change and doing it all with a sense of leading a team of willing participants is complex enough. Doing it for four lessons a day, five times a week makes it seem nigh on impossible. One of the key tools you use to create these masterpieces is your language choice and being able to articulate the reasons behind your choices will be of incredible benefit to your mentee.

<table>
<tr><th colspan="2">Teachers' Standards</th></tr>
<tr><td colspan="2">A teacher must:
Plan and teach well-structured lessons<ul><li>impart knowledge and develop understanding through effective use of lesson time</li><li>promote a love of learning and children's intellectual curiosity
set homework and plan other out-of-class activities to consolidate and extend the knowledge and understanding pupils have acquired</li><li>reflect systematically on the effectiveness of lessons and approaches to teaching</li><li>contribute to the design and provision of an engaging curriculum within the relevant subject area(s).</li></ul></td></tr>
<tr><th colspan="2">Early Career Framework</th></tr>
<tr><td>Learn that...

1.Effective teaching can transform pupils' knowledge, capabilities and beliefs about learning.

2. Effective teachers introduce new material in steps, explicitly linking new ideas to what has been previously studied and learned.

3. Modelling helps pupils understand new processes and ideas; good models make abstract ideas concrete and accessible.</td><td>Learn how to...

Plan effective lessons, by:
• Using modelling, explanations and scaffolds, acknowledging that novices need more structure early in a domain.
• Enabling critical thinking and problem solving by first teaching the necessary foundational content knowledge.
• Removing scaffolding only when pupils are achieving a high degree of success in applying previously taught material.
• Providing sufficient opportunity for pupils to</td></tr>
</table>

4. Guides, scaffolds and worked examples can help pupils apply new ideas; but should be gradually removed as pupil expertise increases. 5. Explicitly teaching pupils metacognitive strategies linked to subject knowledge, including how to plan, monitor and evaluate, supports independence and academic success. 6. Questioning is an essential tool for teachers; questions can be used for many purposes, including to check pupils' prior knowledge, assess understanding and break down problems. 7. High-quality classroom talk can support pupils to articulate key ideas, consolidate understanding and extend their vocabulary. 8. Practice is an integral part of effective teaching; ensuring pupils have repeated opportunities to practise, with appropriate guidance and support, increases success. 9. Paired and group activities can increase pupil success, but	consolidate and practise applying new knowledge and skills. • Breaking tasks down into constituent components when first setting up independent practice (e.g. using tasks that scaffold pupils through meta-cognitive and procedural processes). Make good use of expositions, by: • Starting expositions at the point of current pupil understanding. • Combining a verbal explanation with a relevant graphical representation of the same concept or process, where appropriate. • Using concrete representation of abstract ideas (e.g. making use of analogies, metaphors, examples and non-examples). Model effectively, by: • Narrating thought processes when modelling to make explicit how experts think (e.g. asking questions aloud that pupils should consider when working independently and drawing pupils' attention to

to work together effectively pupils need guidance, support and practice. 10. How pupils are grouped is also important; care should be taken to monitor the impact of groupings on pupil attainment, behaviour and motivation. 11. Homework can improve pupil outcomes, particularly for older pupils, but it is likely that the quality of homework and its relevance to main class teaching is more important than the amount set.	links with prior knowledge). • Making the steps in a process memorable and ensuring pupils can recall them (e.g. naming them, developing mnemonics, or linking to memorable stories). • Exposing potential pitfalls and explaining how to avoid them. Stimulate pupil thinking and check for understanding, by: • Planning activities around what you want pupils to think hard about. • Including a range of types of questions in class discussions to extend and challenge pupils (e.g. by modelling new vocabulary or asking pupils to justify answers). • Providing appropriate wait time between question and response where more developed responses are required. • Considering the factors that will support effective collaborative or paired work (e.g. familiarity with routines, whether pupils have the necessary prior knowledge and how pupils are grouped). • Providing scaffolds for pupil talk to increase the focus and rigour of dialogue.

Discussion

Communication in the classroom takes many forms. Instructions, explanations, praise and admonishments may be the first few that come to mind, but the constructs of what we say are so nuanced it may seem impenetrable at first for a mentee to appreciate its complexities. After years of teaching, you will know how to use paralanguage to your advantage, possibly without even realising it consciously. You alter your pitch, volume and speed as well as the obvious selection of vocabulary to convey information. Beyond this, there is also a layer of physical communication you use to orchestrate smooth lessons and impart information.

Koch (2017) identified four main roles of adults in early years' classes, that of mentor, nurturer, controller and playmate. When looking at variations in prosody (defined by the Oxford reference dictionary as 'the qualities of speech involving loudness, pitch, rhythm, and tempo'), she noted varied combinations used to emphasise the role taken on by the adult. When conveying the role of mentor, the teacher's pitch was low, speed was slow, and talk was at a medium volume. This combination infers a calm, controlled and experienced stance to the children. When conveying a nurturing role, the teacher would use a higher pitch and softer tone, speaking slowly. This would give the effect of being gentle and reassuring to the child. When a controlling voice was needed (in instances where behaviour needed to be checked), a low tone at high volume and a fast speed was used. Finally, when the role of playmate was adopted, the teacher used a high pitch, medium volume and medium speed, presumably consciously mimicking the voices of the children in EYFS that were being interacted with. If we were to watch ourselves back on a recording, we too would notice we adopt different prosodic values at different points during the day. Whilst it is difficult to break them down into the components of volume, tone, pitch and speed without watching your recorded self, it is perhaps easier to think of which of the four roles you frequently adopt. Discussing with mentees the impression they are trying to convey may be a way into a conversation about prosody. Combined with a discussion on other elements of paralanguage and vocabulary choice, it could be a really beneficial teaching point as it is a common mistake for inexperienced teachers to wish to appear friendly and as a peer to pupils which can cause problems at a later date.

Another element of communication which is difficult to teach to a mentee is how body language contributes to communication. The combination of gesture (kinesic) and space (proxemic) can be combined to convey messages which reinforce or add to what is being communicated verbally. We can to some extent, control the classroom environment. Beyond fixed details such as the walls and furniture, we have control over the positioning of workspaces, what is displayed and to a limited degree to the smell, temperature and volume of our classroom. Possibly without even realising it, we are telling our pupils something about ourselves. Our facial expressions, eye movements and gestures can be used to emphasise what we are teaching or be used like a second conversation with an individual whilst we try not to disturb the flow of teaching for others. A further layer is where we choose to position ourselves in the classrooms, walking to stand behind a child who is distracted may be all that is needed to get them focused again, working with a group but having your back to the wall can ensure you maintain class control. You may have a mentee who has an innate ability to optimise their use of space in the classroom, but most likely a conversation about these tips would be beneficial. Castaner, Camerino et al (2011) observed new and experienced PE teachers in a secondary school and found that experienced teachers used kinesic and proxemic paralanguage less, but with a much more precise intention than newer teachers. It was also evident that newer teachers had extraneous movement due to nerves – something which we know children notice. Having a specific conversation about all elements of paralanguage and then asking your mentee to observe this in other teachers may enlighten their understanding of something that is often overlooked.

The most obvious form of communication – that of verbal constructs – can be observed at different levels of detail. At the surface level, we can talk about teacher talk in terms such as open and closed questions, explanations and instructions. Another way to categorise conversation is to identify the patterns of initiation-response-feedback (IRF) in classroom talk. Alexander (2008), stated that there were five kinds of talk for teaching: rote (drilling of facts), recitation (questions which stimulated recall), exposition (telling pupils what to do), discussion (the exchange of ideas), and dialogue (a common understanding developed through guided discussion of concepts). In the classroom, we may see this last talk type most commonly used in guided reading lessons. Tennent et al (2016) has some excellent transcripts of this type of talk for mentees to look at and base their planning on. Known as dialogic talk, Alexander explains that there are five principles to adhere to. They are that dialogic talk is collective, reciprocal, cumulative, supportive and purposeful. Whilst teaching entirely through this approach (known as dialogic teaching) may not feel like something that fits in with your stance, you will undoubtedly use many of these principles at times. There is much to be gained by analysing the types of talk you use most frequently. Considering when they are used (in which lessons, at which point in the lesson for example) will again give you clarity about what works and what can be passed on to your mentee.

By 2018, Alexander had refined his explanation of dialogic teaching into four components, with dialogic talk embedded within. Understanding the justification for the talk (for example political or pedagogical), the principles (communicative, reciprocal), the chosen repertoire (groupings and talk type), and indicators (ideals by which to judge high quality dialogic teaching), were the four components of the approach.

For the purposes of supporting mentees, a focus on observing repertoires may be most insightful to see how talk is used across the school day. Alexander's repertoires include:

(1) Interactive settings whole class – group work (teacher led) – group work (pupil led) – teacher to pupil – pupil to pupil

(2) Everyday talk Transactional – Expository – Interrogatory – Exploratory – Expressive – Evaluative

(3) Learning talk Narrate – Explain – Speculate – Imagine –Explore – Analyse – Evaluate – Question – Justify – Discuss – Argue – Listen

(4) Teaching talk Rote – Recitation – Instruction – Exposition – Discussion – Dialogue

(5) Questioning Character Response cue – Participation cue – Wait/thinking time – Feedback – Purpose – Structure

(6) Extending Time to think Say more – Revoice – Rephrase/repeat – Evidence of reasoning – Challenge or counter-example – Agree/disagree – Add on – Explain what someone else means

(repertoire 6 was developed by Michaels and O'Connor, 2012)

Interweaving all these elements happens across a whole term, maybe a whole year, so it is vital mentees don't see it as a checklist for a good lesson to incorporate most or even some. There are probably examples you can think of where just one or two types of repertoire were used and the lesson was excellent. As I have said in every chapter, it is the chance to hear your reasoning behind the choices you make and the explanation for why you discarded what you did that is the vital opportunity your mentee gets from working with you.

Learning Activities

Supporting Trainee Teachers

Observe the class teacher using the teacher talk record sheet. Analyse the different types of language the teacher uses across a typical lesson. If you get a chance to repeat this activity, see how different tasks require different types of talk from the teacher.

Supporting Newly Qualified Teachers

Read Doug Lemov's 'Teach like a Champion 2.0 Field Guide' (2016) and try and incorporate one or two new ideas into your practice. If you can, select ideas that will develop your understanding of classroom talk.

Supporting Early Career Teachers

Visit https://visible-learning.org/hattie-ranking-influences-effect-sizes-learning-achievement/ and investigate some of the influences that have effect sizes over 0.4. Choose one or two that you think fit with your style of teaching and use different ways to structure class groups and/or activities to promote talk and try them out in your class.

Discuss with your mentor how you will measure how successful they are for you- will it be by pupil outcome, by how confident you feel using them, or the culture they create in your classroom?

Growing as a Mentor

Consider all the different ways you communicate throughout a day. Use the teacher talk record sheet as a prompt. Can you articulate for your mentee some of the reasons behind the choices you make? You probably use open questions to get talk started, closed questions to move the lesson forward or to check learning, eye contact, tone of voice, repetition -the use of silence even-amongst many others. Explaining the choices an experienced teacher makes almost subconsciously will prove an invaluable learning opportunity for others.

References

Alexander, R. (2008) Towards dialogic teaching: Rethinking classroom talk, Dialogos, Cambridge

Castañer, M. Camerino, O. Anguera, M. and Johnson, G. (2011) *'Kinesics and proxemics communication of expert and novice PE teachers',* in Quality & quantity. Dordrecht: Springer Science and Business Media LLC, 47(4), pp. 1813–1829.

Koch, A. (2017) Sounds of Education: Teacher Role and Use of Voice in Interactions with Young Children in IJEC (2017) 49 pp57–72

Lemov, D., Hernandez, J. Kim, J. (2016) Teach like a champion 2.0 field guide: a practical resource to make the 62 techniques your own, John Wiley and Sons, San Francisco

Michaels, S., and C. O'Connor. 2012. Talk Science Primer. TERC, Cambridge MA

Oxford Reference Dictionary https://www.oxfordreference.com/

Tennent, W. Reedy, D. Hobsbaum, A. Gamble, N. (2016) Guided reading- layers of meaning, UCL, London

Teacher Talk Observation Form

	Time (minutes)									
Type of talk	1	2	3	4	5	6	7	8	9	10
Closed Question										
Open Question										
Explanation (verbal only)										
Explanation (with modelling)										
Instruction (task)										
Instruction (organisational)										
Instruction (behavioural)										
Follow up to child comment										
Rephrase child comment										
Ask for expansion										
Behaviour (praise)										
Behaviour (sanction)										
Talking to another adult										
Deliberate pause										
Communication through prosody										
Communication through body language										

You may choose to use this simplified checklist first before creating one based on Alexander's Repertoires

5 ADAPTING YOUR TEACHING

Overview

Once you have taught for a substantial period of time, you know that every child can progress, every child can succeed, but despite your best efforts not every child will hit every milestone of the curriculum exactly as it is outlined. The essence, though, of every great teacher is that they have high aspirations for every child and an intention for them to reach their full potential. To do this, we continually adapt our teaching and incorporate new techniques, resources and approaches. Being critically reflective of what works and what doesn't in your context, and being brave enough to change systems which have worked in the past for different children because something might work better in the current class is, I believe, the distinction between a good teacher and a great one. Demonstrating to your mentee that you are responsive to the needs of the children, and that it is no failure to abandon a method of intervention or delivery if you believe another one will work better, may be the one single most important thing you can do. The vital part is informing them how you came to these conclusions and how to evaluate techniques for their potential.

<table>
<tr><th colspan="2">Teachers' Standards</th></tr>
<tr><td colspan="2">A teacher must:
Adapt teaching to respond to the strengths and needs of all pupils
• know when and how to differentiate appropriately, using approaches which enable pupils to be taught effectively
• have a secure understanding of how a range of factors can inhibit pupils' ability to learn, and how best to overcome these
• demonstrate an awareness of the physical, social and intellectual development of children, and know how to adapt teaching to support pupils' education at different stages of development
• have a clear understanding of the needs of all pupils, including those with special educational needs; those of high ability; those with English as an additional language; those with disabilities; and be able to use and evaluate distinctive teaching approaches to engage and support them..</td></tr>
<tr><th colspan="2">Early Career Framework</th></tr>
<tr><td>Learn that...

1. Pupils are likely to learn at different rates and to require different levels and types of support from teachers to succeed.

2. Seeking to understand pupils' differences, including their different levels of prior knowledge and potential barriers to learning, is an essential part of teaching.</td><td>Learn how to...

Develop an understanding of different pupil needs, by:
• Identifying pupils who need new content further broken down.
• Making use of formative assessment.
• Working closely with the Special Educational Needs Co-ordinator (SENCO) and special education professionals and the Designated Safeguarding Lead.</td></tr>
</table>

3. Adapting teaching in a responsive way, including by providing targeted support to pupils who are struggling, is likely to increase pupil success. 4. Adaptive teaching is less likely to be valuable if it causes the teacher to artificially create distinct tasks for different groups of pupils or to set lower expectations for particular pupils. 5. Flexibly grouping pupils within a class to provide more tailored support can be effective, but care should be taken to monitor its impact on engagement and motivation, particularly for low attaining pupils. 6. There is a common misconception that pupils have distinct and identifiable learning styles. This is not supported by evidence and attempting to tailor lessons to learning styles is unlikely to be beneficial. 7. Pupils with special educational needs or disabilities are likely to require additional or adapted support; working closely with colleagues, families	• Using the SEND Code of Practice, which provides additional guidance on supporting pupils with SEND effectively. Provide opportunity for all pupils to experience success, by: • Adapting lessons, whilst maintaining high expectations for all, so that all pupils have the opportunity to meet expectations. • Balancing input of new content so that pupils master important concepts. • Making effective use of Teaching Assistants. Meet individual needs without creating unnecessary workload, by: • Making use of well-designed resources (e.g. textbooks). • Planning to connect new content with pupils' existing knowledge or providing additional pre-teaching if pupils lack critical knowledge. • Building in additional practice or removing unnecessary expositions. • Reframing questions to provide greater scaffolding or greater stretch.

and pupils to understand barriers and identify effective strategies is essential.	• Considering carefully whether intervening within lessons with individuals and small groups would be more efficient and effective than planning different lessons for different groups of pupils. Group pupils effectively, by: • Applying high expectations to all groups, and ensuring all pupils have access to a rich curriculum. • Changing groups regularly, avoiding the perception that groups are fixed. • Ensuring that any groups based on attainment are subject specific

Discussion

Now more than ever, the teaching profession is evidence informed. The inception of the Education Endowment Foundation Toolkit gives instant information as to the cost, strength of evidence base and months of progress, for a wide range of interventions. Hattie's (2009) book 'Visible Learning' and associated website provides meta analyses of over 800 factors that have an effect on student achievement. The vital difference between these sources and previous research, is that they are both collations of meta-analyses, i.e. they are data collected from a wide range of research and 'averaged' in a way. Hattie's term 'zone of desired effects' indicates when an activity gives significant enough improvement to make the kind of difference we would want to see. The EEF site gives us the valuable information of how many months progress a child could be expected to make whilst on the programme – an opportunity in some cases to 'catch up' with the cohort.

In the past, I have selected interventions based on these information sites. When faced with no curriculum budget to buy resources, but a need to 'close the gap' for children who were close to meeting the end of key stage, I searched through both resources and found Reciprocal Reading as a possible solution. With no resources beyond what we already had in school and a bit of photocopying, I was able to set up this programme for a core of children and a Teaching Assistant, and the progress I had hoped for was indeed made. Years later, I was able to redesign the same concept to help a much larger group of children who were reluctant readers. This is an important point- once you select one of these interventions, as an experienced teacher you may take what you need from it and adapt it to fit your situation. Supporting new and recently qualified teachers is about bridging the gap for them between what they have read about and how they could apply it in their classroom. Having the confidence to do that, and perhaps the insight into what will and won't work, is the role of the mentor. I am not saying disregard your mentees ideas if they haven't worked for you- we all teach differently- but some pointers as to the pitfalls may be welcome. It is easy to be cynical now about the way schools adopted VAK learning styles, or Edward de Bono's thinking hats, but we have to remember they were hoped at the time to improve learning. We now know much more about how the brain works, as discussed in Chapter 2, and in some ways I can see how misunderstanding dual coding twenty years ago could have been what we understood to be visual learning; and the idea of viewing one problem from many different viewpoints (or hats) is an interesting approach to creativity, although applying to primary school classrooms was nigh on impossible. My point is that we need to be willing to try new techniques if we genuinely believe they might help a group, but at the same time learn from our past mistakes (as a profession) and make sure there is evidence behind our choices.

One of the most significant discussions to have with your mentee is that of differentiation vs scaffolding. Differentiation was about providing different tasks, often with different learning objectives to groups of children. Whether or not this was ethically fair, it worked fairly well within the system of levels. If the whole class were writing a story, children working at level 3 might be asked to add adjectives to their writing, at level 4 they were asked to write in paragraphs and those aspiring to be level 5 would include a wide range of sentence structures. The reams of paperwork that were generated when this was combined with APP started to reveal what a nonsense it was for teachers to try to teach one input with so many different aims embedded and track 32 different sets of statements. Differentiation in this form was supposed to be laid to rest with the introduction of the new curriculum. Unbelievably, it is still appearing in some schools and is in fact one of the reasons I decided to write this book. I feel we are doing all our trainee and Newly Qualified Teachers (and those that are more experienced but keep up to date with educational developments) an enormous disservice by modelling this in the classroom when they have been taught how to scaffold instead, let alone the children in our schools. It's important to describe what differentiation was for context, but if you are not already scaffolding instead, then maybe this is a chance for your mentee to teach you something.

The approach of scaffolding (where one objective is intended for the whole group), is no easier to plan for, but much easier to deliver in the lesson. When all the children in the class are working towards the same end point, ALL teacher talk is relevant to them. Gone are the days of one group at a time sitting with the teacher whilst the others work, then a frantic swap around so that the teacher has done more work than the children by the end of the lesson. Scaffolding stems from the intentions of the 2014 curriculum, which makes clear that 'teachers should set high expectations for all pupils' (p.8) and the shift from working through levels to reaching age related expectations. The difference here is that whilst levels could continue to be worked on for two, sometimes three years, a system of planning a curriculum by age group means that objectives were covered for one year and built upon by a deeper objective the following year. Missing one objective therefore equates to a gap in the foundations that are required to build upon.

There is little doubt that those that wrote the curriculum did not put as much thought into provision for those with special educational needs. It took several years for acknowledgement that there should be exceptions to the requirements for meeting the end of Key Stage 2 (e.g. those with hypermobility were at one point still expected to pass the statement for handwriting to achieve ARE), and many local authorities and academies spent countless hours creating progression statements to demonstrate progress for children who had no way of accessing the curriculum for their year group. Your school may have their own statements for your mentee to use. Regardless, they should be supported by their SENDCo for any children that are working far below the expectations expected for their year group.

Removing the ceiling on what children can achieve is another aspect where the new curriculum has changed classroom practice. When working with levels, children were assigned a task, often before the lesson itself. Now, in programmes of study such as the White Rose Maths scheme, the lesson is constructed so that all pupils can master concepts and extend their learning to a greater depth. This is a mind shift that was significant as we moved between curriculums, but hopefully seems natural now. Your mentee may not have the bad habits those of us who worked under the previous curriculum had, and you may find that adapting teaching is an area where we can learn from them.

Learning Activities

Supporting Trainee Teachers

Read this blog by David Lowbridge-Ellis on differentiation: https://www.teachertoolkit.co.uk/2018/10/15/ditch-differentiation/. As you observe lessons, identify how your mentor is supporting the majority of children to access the same teaching point. How are the children scaffolded and extended within one shared goal?

Supporting Newly Qualified Teachers

Download and read the Education Endowment Foundation recommendations on how best to deploy Teaching Assistants. https://educationendowmentfoundation.org.uk/public/files/Publications/Teaching_Assistants/TA_RecommendationsSummary.pdf Discuss with your mentor how teaching assistants are used in the school and any effective strategies you could try in your own class.

Supporting Early Career Teachers

Watch these videos on how to scaffold and deepen maths tasks. Consider one of your own lessons and compare the strategies and vocabulary used. Do you put limits on what some children are able to show you based on the task you have given them?
https://www.youtube.com/watch?v=jiEq4yIwgbs
https://www.youtube.com/watch?v=Zv-uhCkLQ1Y

Growing as a Mentor

Consider the techniques you use to scaffold learners and cater for different needs in your class. Read 'Visible Learning' by Hattie (2009) and see how your usual methods are rated. Is there anything with a greater effect size you could try or recommend to others? If you are a Maths, English or Science lead there are subject specific versions of this which may assist you in creating whole school impact.

References

DfE (2013) The National Curriculum in England, available at https://assets.publishing.service.gov.uk/government/uploads/system/uploads/attachment_data/file/425601/PRIMARY_national_curriculum.pdf

Education Endowment Foundation Toolkit, available at https://educationendowmentfoundation.org.uk/evidence-summaries/teaching-learning-toolkit/

Hattie, J. (2009) Visible Learning, Routledge, Oxfordshire

Hood et al, (2017) 'No evidence to back learning styles' in The Guardian, available at https://www.theguardian.com/education/2017/mar/12/no-evidence-to-back-idea-of-learning-styles

The de Bono Group (2019) Six Thinking Hats available at https://www.debonogroup.com/services/core-programs/six-thinking-hats/

Visible Learning, available at https://visible-learning.org/hattie-ranking-influences-effect-sizes-learning-achievement/

White Rose Maths resources available at https://whiterosemaths.com/

6 ASSESSMENT

Overview

Whether you agree with national testing or not, whether you prefer formative or summative assessment and whatever your opinion on comparing countries' performance on a global stage, assessment is interwoven into every level of our job. Understanding the historical context of assessment in our school system, and the political influences over the years will, at least, help you justify the why of the assessments you are using in your school. This is possibly the most divisive of topics you will address with your mentee as the impact on workload and the extent to which assessments are perceived as useful by the class teacher is a hot topic for discussion. Being well-informed of current trends alongside what is common in the schools you know of is probably the most important aspect of preparing to support them in this area.

<table>
<tr><th colspan="2">Teachers' Standards</th></tr>
<tr><td colspan="2">A teacher must:
Make accurate and productive use of assessment
<ul>
<li>know and understand how to assess the relevant subject and curriculum areas, including statutory assessment requirements</li>
<li>make use of formative and summative assessment to secure pupils' progress</li>
<li>use relevant data to monitor progress, set targets, and plan subsequent lessons</li>
<li>give pupils regular feedback, both orally and through accurate marking, and encourage pupils to respond to the feedback.</li>
</ul></td></tr>
<tr><th colspan="2">Early Career Framework</th></tr>
<tr><td>Learn that...

1.Effective assessment is critical to teaching because it provides teachers with information about pupils' understanding and needs.

2. Good assessment helps teachers avoid being over-influenced by potentially misleading factors, such as how busy pupils appear.

3. Before using any assessment, teachers should be clear about the decision it will be used to support and be able to justify its use.</td>
<td>Learn how to...

Avoid common assessment pitfalls, by:
• Planning formative assessment tasks linked to lesson objectives and thinking ahead about what would indicate understanding (e.g. by using hinge questions to pinpoint knowledge gaps).
• Drawing conclusions about what pupils have learned by looking at patterns of performance over a number of assessments (e.g. appreciating that assessments draw inferences about learning from performance).
• Choosing, where possible,</td></tr>
</table>

4. To be of value, teachers use information from assessments to inform the decisions they make; in turn, pupils must be able to act on feedback for it to have an effect. 5. High-quality feedback can be written or verbal; it is likely to be accurate and clear, encourage further effort, and provide specific guidance on how to improve. 6. Over time, feedback should support pupils to monitor and regulate their own learning. 7. Working with colleagues to identify efficient approaches to assessment is important; assessment can become onerous and have a disproportionate impact on workload.	externally validated materials, used in controlled conditions when required to make summative assessments. Check prior knowledge and understanding during lessons, by: • Using assessments to check for prior knowledge and pre-existing misconceptions. • Structuring tasks and questions to enable the identification of knowledge gaps and misconceptions (e.g. by using common misconceptions within multiple-choice questions). • Prompting pupils to elaborate when responding to questioning to check that a correct answer stems from secure understanding. • Monitoring pupil work during lessons, including checking for misconceptions. Provide high-quality feedback, by: • Focusing on specific actions for pupils and providing time for pupils to respond to feedback. • Appreciating that pupils'

	responses to feedback can vary depending on a range of social factors (e.g. the message the feedback contains or the age of the child). • Scaffolding self-assessment by sharing model work with pupils, highlighting key details. • Thinking carefully about how to ensure feedback is specific and helpful when using peer- or self-assessment. Make marking manageable and effective, by: • Recording data only when it is useful for improving pupil outcomes. • Working with colleagues to identify efficient approaches to marking and alternative approaches to providing feedback (e.g. using whole class feedback or well supported peer- and self-assessment). • Using verbal feedback during lessons in place of written feedback after lessons where possible. • Understanding that written marking is only one form of feedback. • Reducing the opportunity cost of marking (e.g. by using

	abbreviations and codes in written feedback). • Prioritising the highlighting of errors related to misunderstandings, rather than careless mistakes when marking

Discussion

Both formative and summative testing has evolved since the introduction of the National Curriculum in 1989. Up until that point, there were tests such as the 11-plus which featured on the education horizon, but teachers were largely left to keep their own records of spelling scores, homework marks and any other tests they felt necessary.

The introduction of Standard Attainment Testing in 1989 implemented tests for children at the end of Key Stage 1 (7-year-olds), Key Stage 2 (11-year-olds) and Key Stage 3 (14-year-olds). After just two years and outcry from teachers, the government revised their original form to a more slimmed down version. Whilst Key Stage 2 and 3 SATs were scrapped in Wales in 2004, it wasn't until 2008 when the government abolished Key Stage 3 SATs in England. For Key Stage 1, the role of SATs was demoted to only forming part of a teacher assessment judgement and are set to be made only optional in 2023. The science SAT was scrapped in 2009, though there are biennial moderation visits carried out by the government which require a randomised selection of 11-year-olds to complete tests in Chemistry, Biology and Physics. In 2012, the Phonics test was introduced for pupils at the end of Year 1, which they were to re-sit at the end of Year 2 if they did not meet the required pass mark first time around. 2012 also saw the last extended writing test for Key Stage Two, replaced by teacher assessment for writing and a Spelling, Punctuation and Grammar test introduced in its place. The most recent change, in 2016, was an abolition of tiered papers (Level 3-5 and Level 6), and since this time all children have completed the same test, with a standardised scaled score denoting the pass mark each year. At the time of writing, the government has just announced there will be no baseline assessments for Year R as planned in September 2020, though this is still intended for the future. Whilst all teachers have their own opinion on how much they agree or disagree with the amount of teaching time that has to be used to prepare children for these tests, and the extent to which they hinder emotional growth and well-being, summative assessment in some form does have its place. Ensuring that knowledge has been embedded into the long-term memory is something we have often left to these summative assessment points - be that yearly, termly or at the end of a topic.

We are, however, getting better at checking this knowledge in a more efficient way- through interleaving (for an explanation, see Firth, 2018) and retrieval practice through quizzing (Rosenshine, 2012). These opportunities would fall under the summative assessment heading as they take place after the main body of learning, albeit whilst there is still time to use the information gained to plan for further learning opportunities to fill gaps.

The most impactful developments though, have happened in our understanding of formative assessment. Wiliam (2018), likens previous incarnations of formative assessment as that to a pilot flying a plane, who sets off in the intended direction and lands after an hour to see if he arrived where he intended. Instead of assessing when it is almost too late to do anything about it, formative assessment takes place in the moment. Of course, this is made much easier by others changes such as the move to scaffolding rather than differentiation (see Chapter 5), and live marking rather than the triple marking rabbit hole we were trapped in several years ago. Resources such as MathsNoProblem also support teachers by identifying the types of misconceptions pupils might develop in lessons – a really helpful way for new and old teachers alike to mentally prepare what the 'wrong' learning would look like so that it is easier to identify.

Hattie (2009) identifies providing feedback as scoring an impressive 0.73, sitting well within the zone of desired effects (0.4 is considered notable). He does note that this effect is not just from teachers giving pupils feedback, but also students providing teachers with information about their learning. As with all teaching techniques, finding a way of getting pupils to feed back in a meaningful way which can inform the teacher rather than just a 'busy task' is the key to making the activity worthwhile. Just as we demonstrate what a final piece of art or DT work would look like and model the thought process as we get there, so too do we need to explain to pupils how they would make the judgements to feedback to their teacher. Sherrington and Caviglioli (2020) have an excellent chapter in their 'Walkthrus' book on using responsive teaching to get feedback, as does Lemov (2016) in 'Teach like a Champion'.

The difficulty of gaining the information to *really* know if a pupil has understood is something you will need to model in many different ways across your practice. Discerning whether a child has truly understood a concept, rather than just chanced upon the right answer needs a combination of actual instinct and the experience you bring to the situation. This could be broached by explaining the difference between two similar written answers where the subtleties of what you know about a child makes all the difference. It goes without saying that as teachers who have transitioned between levels and the mastery approach, we have had to learn ourselves how ethereal this judgements can feel at times, and that going back to a topic days or even weeks later can give a different perspective on what we think a child has learned. Hard as it is, demonstrating this fallibility to a new teacher could give their confidence such a boost. To know that every class has children that are harder to assess will support your mentee and give them the confidence to make judgements. If you have had the opportunity to attend moderation meetings, for your own subject or for the end of Key Stage One and Two assessments, you will possibly be able to describe the influence knowledge *about* a pupil or context has on assessment decisions even more explicitly. Judgements about the level of support given (word banks, models), autonomy around selecting answers (e.g. multiple choice or not) and context (e.g. applying knowledge from one subject in another) all add or detract to what is seen as evidence.

Modelling what we do with the information gained from assessment is also an important aspect of mentoring. To a novice, the juggernaut of information gathered through various types of assessment may seem to immense to be of any use. Dividing this information into three strands and making it explicit what you do with each may make it seem less daunting.

Firstly, we have that general assessment of how a lesson went, did we cover what we needed to, did the children engage as we expected, complete activities to the relevant depth we had hoped for? If this is the case, then this broad assessment means we can move on to the next stage in our programme of study. If not, the decision is made as to whether the same concept needs to be taught again with a different tactic, or if a few minutes at the beginning of the next lesson to address misconceptions will be enough. There may also be a few children who need something specific which you will also arrange. Didau (2016) gives us pause to think when he states, 'all that formative assessment within lessons can tell us is what pupils *haven't* learned, never what they *have* learned' (p.289). If your school uses whole class feedback forms, this would be a perfect opportunity to analyse with your mentee how you record this information. If not, an example can be found at the end of this chapter.

The second strand of assessment may be the record keeping of who has understood a concept at the level expected for the task – we are able to say they can do it today, but not yet able to say they 'know' this, and that make take the form of quiz answers, exit tickets, conversations in the lesson. Dependent on your school context, you may or may not be expected to record keep in a specific format. It's important to stress to mentees that you are not always able to make a decision for every child in every lesson, and neither should they feel they have to. When considering how much of a mentee's working memory in a lesson is taken up ensuring the correct delivery of what they have planned, assisting them with completing assessments may take the form of modelling how you deploy other adults to make observations, how you focus on a small group of children at times or how you collect information in written form to look at later.

The third strand is the assessment we are accountable for to those outside our classroom. Keeping notes across the year for Parents' Evenings and pupil progress meetings is another element which can seem overwhelming as a task initially, so again sharing any efficient ways you have of doing this will ease this pressure. Participating in moderating assessment tasks, even reading and understanding mark schemes for external or bought in assessments well in advance of carrying them out are useful tasks to set your mentee to make the assessments themselves run smoothly and give more accurate information. Hopefully your pupil progress measures are realistic and achievable, supporting your mentee with understanding how trajectories are predicted and how judgements on the previous year have been decided will give them a strong starting point for working with each pupil to achieve their full potential.

Learning Activities

Supporting Trainee Teachers

Begin to investigate the statutory assessment points in the primary phase. Look at the early learning goals for EYFS here: http://www.lancsngfl.ac.uk/curriculum/assessment/download/file/Early%20Learning%20%20Goals.pdf

View the resources relating to the Year 1 phonics check here: https://www.gov.uk/government/publications/phonics-screening-check-sample-materials-and-training-video,

and some examples of end of KS2 assessments (SATs) here: https://www.gov.uk/government/collections/national-curriculum-assessments-practice-materials#key-stage-2-past-papers

Supporting Newly Qualified Teachers

Listen to this podcast from Dylan Wiliams on the topic of embedding formative assessment in your classroom: https://educationendowmentfoundation.org.uk/news/trialled-and-tested-podcast-embedding-formative-assessment/

Investigate what constitutes meeting Age Related Expectations in the year group above and below your own. Look at maths and writing, but also find out about the foundation subjects and reading too.

Supporting Early Career Teachers

Read the governmental briefing paper on assessments in England. It also has a brief overview of how assessment has developed over the years. You can download the paper here: https://commonslibrary.parliament.uk/research-briefings/cbp-7980/

Growing as a Mentor

PISA results are often talked about in the press and used to compare educational models from around the world. Gain insight into its role in informing and shaping educational reform by looking at the information on these two pages: http://www.oecd.org/pisa/aboutpisa/
and http://www.oecd.org/pisa/pisafaq/

References

Dabell, J. (2019) Maths misconceptions: Multiplying by 10 available at https://mathsnoproblem.com/blog/teaching-tips/maths-misconceptions-multiplying-ten/

Didau, D. (2016) What if everything you knew about education was wrong? Crown House, Wales

Firth, J. (2018) *The application of spacing and interleaving approaches in the classroom,* in Impact magazine, available at https://impact.chartered.college/article/firth-spacing-interleaving-classroom/

Lemov, D. Hernandez, J. Kim, J. (2016) Teach like a champion 2.0 field guide: a practical resource to make the 62 techniques your own, John Wiley and Sons, San Francisco

Rosenshine, B. (2012) *Principles of instruction: research-based strategies that all teachers should know,* in American Educator, American Federation of Teachers, AFL-CIO, 36(1), p12.

Sherrington, T. Caviglioli. O. (2020) Walkthrus, John Catt Educational, Woodbridge

Wiliam, D. (2018) What do we mean by Assessment for Learning? presentation available at https://www.youtube.com/watch?v=q-myBw36_DA

Whole Class Feedback Form

General Misconceptions:	New examples to use to rectify:
SPAG points to pick up:	Good Examples to Celebrate:
Specific children and work needed (when, named adult):	Notes:

7 MANAGING BEHAVIOUR

Overview

If you work in a school where behaviour is well-managed, this may seem like an easy topic to address. Equally, if you are a teacher who is naturally adept at behaviour management you may find it difficult to be explicit about what exactly your thought processes are in tricky situations. One of the common complaints about teacher training is that behaviour management has not been given enough time on the course programme to empower Newly Qualified Teachers to run their own class. This in turn can exacerbate any problems as children are quick to sense a weak spot and capitalise on it. Compounding this issue is the growing amount of complex behavioural issues that we are seeing coming through the school gates and the lack of well-funded social support meaning that the brunt of the issues are now being taken on by school leadership teams. Of course every child and every situation is different, and one of the best pieces of advice for your mentee would be to seek help as soon as they feel they might need it, rather than battling on for fear of hearing 'they behave for me'. However, the basics of behaviour management can be discussed in preparation, leaving more brain space for addressing the complex cases.

<table>
<tr><th colspan="2">Teachers' Standards</th></tr>
<tr><td colspan="2">A teacher must:
Manage behaviour effectively to ensure a good and safe learning environment<ul><li>have clear rules and routines for behaviour in classrooms, and take responsibility for promoting good and courteous behaviour both in classrooms and around the school, in accordance with the school's behaviour policy</li><li>have high expectations of behaviour, and establish a framework for discipline with a range of strategies, using praise, sanctions and rewards consistently and fairly</li><li>manage classes effectively, using approaches which are appropriate to pupils' needs in order to involve and motivate them</li><li>maintain good relationships with pupils, exercise appropriate authority, and act decisively when necessary.</li></ul></td></tr>
<tr><th colspan="2">Early Career Framework</th></tr>
<tr><td>Learn that...

1.Establishing and reinforcing routines, including through positive reinforcement, can help create an effective learning environment.

2. A predictable and secure environment benefits all pupils, but is particularly valuable for pupils with special educational needs.

3. The ability to self-regulate one's emotions affects pupils'</td><td>Learn how to...

Develop a positive, predictable and safe environment for pupils, by:
• Establishing a supportive and inclusive environment with a predictable system of reward and sanction in the classroom.
• Working alongside colleagues as part of a wider system of behaviour management (e.g. recognising responsibilities and understanding the right to assistance and training from</td></tr>
</table>

ability to learn, success in school and future lives. 4. Teachers can influence pupils' resilience and beliefs about their ability to succeed, by ensuring all pupils have the opportunity to experience meaningful success. 5. Building effective relationships is easier when pupils believe that their feelings will be considered and understood. 6. Pupils are motivated by intrinsic factors (related to their identity and values) and extrinsic factors (related to reward). 7. Pupils' investment in learning is also driven by their prior experiences and perceptions of success and failure.	senior colleagues). • Giving manageable, specific and sequential instructions. • Checking pupils' understanding of instructions before a task begins. • Using consistent language and non-verbal signals for common classroom directions. • Using early and least-intrusive interventions as an initial response to low level disruption. • Responding quickly to any behaviour or bullying that threatens emotional safety. Establish effective routines and expectations, by: • Creating and explicitly teaching routines in line with the school ethos that maximise time for learning (e.g. setting and reinforcing expectations about key transition points). • Practising routines at the beginning of the school year. • Reinforcing routines (e.g. by articulating the link between time on task and success). Build trusting relationships, by: • Liaising with parents, carers and colleagues to better

	understand pupils' individual circumstances and how they can be supported to meet high academic and behavioural expectations. • Responding consistently to pupil behaviour. Motivate pupils, by: • Supporting pupils to master challenging content, which builds towards long-term goals. • Providing opportunities for pupils to articulate their long-term goals and helping them to see how these are related to their success in school. • Helping pupils to journey from needing extrinsic motivation to being motivated to work intrinsically

Discussion

I have worked in a school who had their behaviour system perfectly attuned to a conducive learning environment, and at a school where it was actively destructive towards learning. If you are thinking your school is more like the latter, stop reading this book and save yourself by starting to search for a new position. No matter how outstanding you are as a teacher, if the system beyond your classroom is broken, if you are not supported by SLT and children have no boundaries or sanctions outside of your room, it is a losing battle. It is never more vital that all the adults share the same opinion as it is when envisioning the behaviour aspect of school culture. You probably have experience of the teacher that is too over friendly with pupils, lets them run when everyone else asks them to walk, or call out when everyone is supposed to listen. Whilst this may stem from their own insecurities or need to be liked, you will know full well that it makes your job, and that of your colleagues, harder. Tom Bennett was commissioned by the DfE in 2017 to review behaviour in schools across the UK, and he found that the biggest challenges teachers faced were:

- inconsistencies between staff and departments
- a lack of clarity of vision, or poor communication of that vision to staff or students
- a lack of sufficient in-school classroom management skills
- poorly calibrated, or low expectations
- inadequate orientation for new staff or students
- staff over-burdened by workload, and therefore unable to direct behaviour effectively
- unsuitably skilled staff in charge of pivotal behaviour roles
- remote, unavailable, or over-occupied leadership

(Bennett, 2017, p.9)

Children need boundaries to feel safe. There has been much debate around the schools known to be strict (or warm-strict as they describe themselves), and many criticise their approach without really delving into its intentions. Rousseau (1762) -who did not bring up his own children- claimed that children needed 'no other guide than [their] own reason', and unbelievably, this idea does still permeate some behaviour policies today. The theorists John Dewey and Paul Friere both add weight to this position as they promoted the notion of democracy (Dewey) and anti-authoritarian approaches (Friere). The assumption that children will 'pick up' socially acceptable behaviour does seem at odds with our naturally selfish, egocentric selves. Just as Sweller explains problem-solving in a curriculum context is impossible without knowledge, so too is managing one's own behaviour without being

directly taught the skills needed to do so. Bennett's (2017) review found eight traits common to those schools which were most successful. They were:
1) attention to detail
2) staff engagement
3) consistent practice
4) visible leaders
5) detailed expectations
6) clarity of culture
7) high staff support
8) all students matter

(Bennett, 2017, p.7)

If children know what you expect and where you stand, they will feel secure. They might not be able to articulate it, but you will see it in their behaviour. Even if they are showing you by rallying against it and pushing the boundaries, just like a small child they are testing to see where they are and knowing you care enough to draw a line when needed. Warm-strict schools, such as Michaela, are like the best parents. In her chapter, 'We believe in Authority', Staw (2020) explains that the school looks at the little details – silence in the corridors is one which gets the most press – and the bigger details follow on from this. It means that a disruptive child can break the rules by talking in the corridor rather than bring in a knife to get the attention they crave (which ultimately is what often motivates poor behaviour). She explains that if expectation and consistency permeate the whole school, Staw says, 'inconsistency is extremely stressful for children' (p.89).

As a mentor, making explicit to trainee teachers that establishing thc right relationship from the start is crucial. If they model their behaviours on yours, the children will see them as someone to be respected, if they sit and chat or overshare, the children will see them as a peer. If you are mentoring a Newly Qualified Teacher, the most important time to have the behaviour discussion is before those first few days with their new class.

The phrase 'Don't smile until Christmas', is much maligned – and if it is taken at face value, then it should be. But I think the intention behind it is to emphasise how important setting out your rules, routines and expectations are. Newly Qualified Teachers need to establish their persona and make it clear what is acceptable behaviour from the very first day. They need to feel confident that it is ok to spend more time establishing routines for the start, end and transition between lessons in those first few days than anything else. They need assurance that dedicating time to it now will reap endless benefits later. As Tom Bennett outlined in his researchED talk in 2016, routines save time, deter poor behaviour choices, provide reinforcement of what is considered the social norm in the classroom and free up thinking time. If children know how to tidy away, move between rooms or get ready for learning, your NQT won't be hoarse by half term and children's working memory can be dedicated to what content is being learned. Sherrington and Caviglioli's (2020) book entitled 'Walkthrus' has step-by-step guides on how to establish classroom conditions for learning through behaviour and relationship management and is well worth a new teacher reading.

Mentor experience again is invaluable here- it is worth letting your mentee know that you had days when behaviour was an issue because of bad weather, or an IT failure, or an unexpected visitor to the classroom (human or insect!) disturbed the learning. The difference between you and them is of course that you have a bank of good experiences which far outweigh the bad ones and a hundred challenging situations which you had under control to draw upon.

It's also important to let your mentee know that regularly coming back and 're-setting' the expectations for behaviour can be necessary. It seems ironic that we spend so much time in school thinking about Growth Mindset and Metacognition, and yet sometimes overlook the basic requirements of teaching children to behave well. As Bennett (2019) describes, we need to be an architect of the culture we want to see in our classroom, and that culture doesn't come naturally to all children.

Of course, there will be outliers, children who for one reason or another are outside the parameters of the normal behaviour system in school. Supporting your mentee with these and directing them to the correct help, either within the school or through outside agencies is another significant aspect of being a mentor. There is a lot of help and advice out there for specific issues, for example Dane Norris (2018) has some suggestions for how to deal with children with ADHD. The key, though, when taking this advice to give your mentee the chance to reflect on whether or not it fits in with their beliefs about teaching and their classroom. If they believe strongly in behaviouristic rewards and sanctions, then restorative justice is probably not going to be a natural addition to their skillset. It is perfectly acceptable to feel tremendous sadness for a child who has had a traumatic start in life, or lives with a condition that makes the behaviours expected in school hard, whilst still protecting your own mental health and reaching out for informed support so that your lessons are not continually disrupted, and we have a duty to make sure new teachers know this or they will suffer burn out.

Learning Activities

Supporting Trainee Teachers

Request a copy of the school's behaviour policy (it can also bc found on the school website). To what extent can you see it being carried out on a day to day basis? Make sure you ask for clarity if there are any areas you do not understand as you will be expected to adhere to it when working with groups/ teaching. Find out how the behaviour policy was created and which stakeholders were involved.

Supporting Newly Qualified Teachers

This guide, written by Tom Bennett and published by Unison, is a clear and concise explanation of the key elements of behaviour management. If you are short on time, read page 4 which summarises the top 10 behaviour tips and come back to the rest at a later date. 'Managing Difficult Behaviour in Schools' available at https://www.unison.org.uk/content/uploads/2015/04/On-line-Catalogue22970.pdf

Supporting Early Career Teachers

Watch Managing Behaviour for Learning Q&A with Tom Bennett, an Independent Behaviour Advisor which is available at https://www.youtube.com/watchv=7aDwV6Ny4Pw and make notes on the key questions he asks which are relevant to your practice.

Growing as a Mentor

In 2017 the DfE commissioned a review of behaviour in schools. Although aimed at school leaders, you might want to read it to gain an overview of behaviour in schools across the country. You can read the recommendations from the review here: https://assets.publishing.service.gov.uk/government/uploads/system/uploads/attachment_data/file/602487/Tom_Bennett_Independent_Review_of_Behaviour_in_Schools.pdf

References

Bennett, T. (2017) Creating a Culture: How school leaders can optimise behaviour -Independent Review of Behaviour in Schools, Department for Educations, London available at https://assets.publishing.service.gov.uk/government/uploads/system/uploads/attachment_data/file/602487/Tom_Bennett_Independent_Review_of_Behaviour_in_Schools.pdf

Bennett, T. (2019) Behviour lessons from the best UK schools researchED Netherlands available at https://www.youtube.com/watch?v=H2dodAZu-WQ

Dewey, J (1916) Democracy and Education: An introduction to the philosophy of Education, Macmillan, New York

Friere, P. (1998) Pedagogy of Freedom: Ethics, democracy and civic courage, Rowman and Littlefield, Lanham

Norris, D. (2018) ADHD Behaviour Management – What to do, and What Not to do When they Disrupt your Lesson available at https://www.teachwire.net/news/adhd-behaviour-management-what-to-do-and-what-not-to-do-when-they-disrupt-your-lesson

Rousseau, J. (1762, trans. 1991) Emile, or on Education, Penguin Classics, London

Staw, R. (2020) *'We believe in Authority'* in Birbalsingh, K. ed. (2020) Michaela: The Power of Culture, John Catt Educational, Woodbridge

Sherrington, T. Caviglioli. O. (2020) Walkthrus, John Catt Educational, Woodbridge

Sweller, J. (1988) *Cognitive Load During Problem Solving: Effects on Learning* in Cognitive Science (12) pp257-285

8 THE WIDER ROLE

Overview

There was a time when it was simply expected that teachers ran clubs after school, had a stall at the summer fair and gave up copious amounts of their own time to contribute to the wider life of the school. I am glad that that time has gone; the pressure on working parents to forsake time with their own children to do this and the phenomenal increase in expectations of what can be achieved in a school day often means there is little time left for eating, let alone running craft club on a Thursday after school. It does leave us, though, with the dilemma of how we prove our 'contribution to the wider life of the school' - which sadly can often still be used as the deciding factor for progressing to the upper pay scale. Increasingly, pursuing action research, leading whole school initiatives, or having a mentoring position is a way for teachers to impact on the whole school as part of their job. For less experienced teachers, engaging with outside agencies, parents and the school SENDCo and DSL are the beginnings of participating in the wider network of community that their class sits within.

<table>
<tr><th colspan="2">Teachers' Standards</th></tr>
<tr><td colspan="2">A teacher must:
Fulfil wider professional responsibilities
• make a positive contribution to the wider life and ethos of the school
• develop effective professional relationships with colleagues, knowing how and when to draw on advice and specialist support
• deploy support staff effectively
• take responsibility for improving teaching through appropriate professional development, responding to advice and feedback from colleagues
• communicate effectively with parents with regard to pupils' achievements and well-being.</td></tr>
<tr><th colspan="2">Early Career Framework</th></tr>
<tr><td>Learn that...

1.Effective professional development is likely to be sustained over time, involve expert support or coaching and opportunities for collaboration.

2. Reflective practice, supported by feedback from and observation of experienced colleagues, professional debate, and learning from educational research, is also likely to support improvement.

3. Teachers can make valuable contributions to the wider life of the school in a broad range</td><td>Learn how to...

Develop as a professional, by:
• Engaging in professional development focused on developing an area of practice with clear intentions for impact on pupil outcomes, sustained over time with built-in opportunities for practice.
• Strengthening pedagogical and subject knowledge by participating in wider networks
• Seeking challenge, feedback and critique from mentors and other colleagues in an open and trusting working environment.</td></tr>
</table>

of ways, including by supporting and developing effective professional relationships with colleagues. 4. Building effective relationships with parents, carers and families can improve pupils' motivation, behaviour and academic success. 5. Teaching assistants (TAs) can support pupils more effectively when they are prepared for lessons by teachers, and when TAs supplement rather than replace support from teachers. 6. SENCOs, pastoral leaders, careers advisors and other specialist colleagues also have valuable expertise and can ensure that appropriate support is in place for pupils. 7. Engaging in high-quality professional development can help teachers improve.	• Engaging critically with research and discussing evidence with colleagues. • Reflecting on progress made, recognising strengths and weaknesses and identifying next steps for further improvement. Build effective working relationships, by: • Contributing positively to the wider school culture and developing a feeling of shared responsibility for improving the lives of all pupils within the school. • Seeking ways to support individual colleagues and working as part of a team. • Communicating with parents and carers proactively and making effective use of parents' evenings to engage parents and carers in their children's schooling. Working closely with the SENCO and other professionals supporting pupils with additional needs, making explicit links between interventions delivered outside of lessons with classroom teaching.

	• Sharing the intended lesson outcomes with Teaching Assistants ahead of lessons. • Ensuring that support provided by Teaching Assistants in lessons is additional to, rather than a replacement for, support from the teacher. • Knowing who to contact with any safeguarding concerns. Manage workload and wellbeing, by: • Using and personalising systems and routines to support efficient time and task management. • Understanding the right to support (e.g. to deal with misbehaviour). • Collaborating with colleagues to share the load of planning and preparation and making use of shared resources (e.g. textbooks). • Protecting time for rest and recovery.

Discussion

Being a role model to your mentee with regards to how you direct your Teaching Assistant again needs reflection on *why* you deploy them the way you do. Mentees need to know that experience can vary between having a Teaching Assistant all day, every day, to someone for just a few hours of core subject support a week. Whilst they may have been taught what to expect the role of Teaching Assistant to be (and we have seen the expectations on Teaching Assistants increase a hundredfold over the past 15 years –unlike their pay), the greatest insight from a mentor may be around the ways to carve out a working relationship. It can be daunting for a Newly Qualified Teacher to direct a Teaching Assistant with years of experience; equally it can be frustrating for an excellent Teaching Assistant to feel they are not being used to their full potential due to a lack of consideration as to how they can complement the work of the class teacher. A great starting point to direct mentees to is the Education Endowment Foundation research on 'Making Best use of Teaching Assistants' found online. As a minimum, your mentee needs to be clear when providing Teaching Assistants with:

- Concepts, facts, information being taught
- Skills to be learned, applied, practised or extended
- Intended learning outcomes
- Expected/required feedback.

(EEF, Oct 2018)

Having a successful working relationship with the other adults you work with in school is not something that everyone finds comes naturally to them. The nature of our job means that we generally work quite well on our own, are used to giving instructions that get followed and being the definitive source of knowledge for others. It can be difficult, but worth it, to step back and consider the nature of the relationships you have with those in different roles. Are you expected to direct or lead them, work as equals, act as mentor, coach, be the authority or follow their direction? The language you use not only affirms your role in each of these relationships, but also makes a difference to the outcome of the conversation (see Halliday, 1980, for more on social interpretation of language). The extent to which your choice of register and code is formal or consultative the difference between someone thinking they have been told to do something or asked. Equally, if you choose a register and tone that is too casual or lacks formality, someone might not realise you had actually made a request. We have all been at the receiving end of someone in authority lacking any clarity in their vision; an incompetent middle leader who should be informative but instead relies on informal phrasing and casual code to evade giving answers; or even a peer who uses a register that uses an authoritative tone to the point of rudeness. Explicitly discussing the interactions we have in school (and the different position your mentee is in), will help them build a firm foundation for excellent working relationships going forward.

The fact that you have read this book demonstrates that you are aware of the need for continuous professional development. As teachers, there is a necessity to increase our knowledge regularly across several areas. The quantity of time and necessity to focus on each area, however varies. In the beginning, classroom management and teaching effective lessons dominates our thinking. This is termed by Cochran-Smith and Lytle (1999) as knowledge **in** practice. Whilst training, this is combined with knowledge **for** practice, which takes the form of understanding pedagogical theory and in recent years the accompanying neuroscience. As we become more experienced, our ways of gaining this knowledge evolves. Attending professional development meetings, INSET, informing ourselves by keeping up to date with current educational debates all contribute to this. We can then send this knowledge outwards through leading development, writing blogs and helping less experienced colleagues. Joining the Chartered College of Teaching means access to a huge resource which supports CPD knowledge as it gives access to articles and research on current issues and how other teachers are addressing them. Cochran-Smith and Lytle's third term, knowledge **of** practice, comes from reviewing activities that have happened in the classroom. As a new teacher, this takes the form of observing others, modifying techniques after trying out ideas in our classrooms. This area is also one which can be capitalised on to contribute to the wider needs of the school. Action Research, which is defined in the Glossary for Education Reform as 'a wide variety of evaluative, investigative, and analytical research methods designed to diagnose problems or weaknesses—whether organizational, academic, or instructional—and help educators develop practical solutions to address them quickly and efficiently', can be used to affect change in your own classroom, school or network. Your own research could be into a variety of areas, for example:

- Teaching methods
- Learning strategies
- Evaluative procedures
- Attitudes and values
- Improving teaching skills
- Behaviour management
- Administration

(Cohen et al, 2011 p.344)

The benefit of Action Research as an element of professional development is the high level of satisfaction for the individual who has undertaken it if the findings are seen to have an impact in school. The socio-culturalists Lave and Wenger (1991) suggest that fully participating in such activities help develop out identity – in this case as an expert teacher. Kelly's (2006) opinion of teachers identity is that it is complex and 'facets of such constructions include how teachers interpret their role, the meanings and understandings which they bring to their role, their beliefs and intentions, and so on' (p.513). Whilst completing action research may not be directly linked to mentoring, the in-depth knowledge into a specific area will no doubt improve your practice, and possibly your self-belief, which can only have a positive impact on those you support.

Learning Activities

Supporting Trainee Teachers

Investigate the range of staff development meetings that take place in your setting. Do all staff attend? How is the schedule set and who leads them? Find out who the Designated Safeguarding Lead and Deputy are and ask them to describe what their job entails. Speak to the SENDCo and other key staff members to find out how their roles support the day-to-day network of adults and children in the school.

Supporting Newly Qualified Teachers

Ask to observe a staff member who has a particular strength in a subject you are less confident in. It could be the subject lead, someone else in your year group or a teacher with a real passion for an area. Once you have had a chance to reflect on their lesson, ask them to come and observe you for a short time teaching. If it is a year group partner, you may want to teach the same lesson; if not you might choose a specific part of the lesson or technique that you'd like their feedback on.

Supporting Early Career Teachers

Consider joining Twitter to take advantage of a broad educational community. Follow @ImpactWales for infographics on a wide range of learning issues; @TeacherTapp to keep up to date on current issues in teaching; @CharteredColl for articles and research carried out by teachers; and @VisibleLearning for an insight into the impact of a wide range of teaching techniques.

Growing as a Mentor

Consider your role as a coach and or mentor. What have you been able to give back to the profession in this capacity? If you would like to develop these skills further, read 'Coaching and Mentoring' (Tolhurst, 2010) which is specifically aimed at coaches and mentors working in schools.

References

Cochran-Smith, M. and Lytle, S. (1999) *'Relationships of knowledge and practice: Teacher learning in communities'*, Review of Research in Education, 24 (1), pp249–305

Cohen, L. Manion, L. Morrison, K. (2011) Research Methods in Education, 7th edition, Routledge, Oxfordshire

Education Endowment Foundation (2018) Making Best Use of Teaching Assistants, available at https://educationendowmentfoundation.org.uk/tools/guidance-reports/making-best-use-of-teaching-assistants/#:~:text=Use%20TAs%20to%20help%20pupils,and%20manage%20their%20own%20learning&text=TAs%20should%2C%20for%20example%2C%20be,least%20amount%20of%20help%20first.

Great Schools Partnership (2014) Glossary of Educational Reform available at https://www.edglossary.org/action-research/

Halliday, M. (1980) *Language as social semiotic: The social interpretation of language and meaning*. Language in Society, Edward Arnold, London, 9 (1) pp84-89

Kelly, P. (2006) *What is teacher learning? A socio-cultural perspective*, Oxford Review of Education, 32 (4), pp505-519

Lave, J. Wenger, E. (1991) Situated Learning: Legitimate Peripheral Participation, Cambridge University Press, Cambridge

Tolhurst, C. (2010) The Essential Guide to Coaching and Mentoring, Pearson, Harlow

Wikipedia https://en.wikipedia.org/wiki/Register_(sociolinguistics)

9 PROFESSIONALISM

Overview

Part Two of the Teachers' Standards can be seen as both everything and nothing. Evidencing it in a tangible way for a Performance Management meeting can be difficult, and yet it is impossible to imagine any competent teacher who does not embody these standards in everything they do. From the weighty responsibility of being a representative of the profession, down to the practicality of following school policy, it is the way we conduct ourselves that infers to others what it means to be a teacher. Society wants to trust us; children need to trust us. Some of this is explicit, we can be asked our opinion on topics, we promote tolerance and equality, we even must even consider our persona on social media. Navigating *that* moral maze may be a very specific conversation you or your Headteacher may wish to have with your mentee. But there is a deeper layer – termed the 'hidden curriculum', which refers to how our school values are communicated inferentially, and we portray this through our actions both explicitly and implicitly.

Teachers' Standards
Part Two: Personal and Professional Conduct A teacher is expected to demonstrate consistently high standards of personal and professional conduct. The following statements define the behaviour and attitudes which set the required standard for conduct throughout a teacher's career. Teachers uphold public trust in the profession and maintain high standards of ethics and behaviour, within and outside school, by: • treating pupils with dignity, building relationships rooted in mutual respect, and at all times observing proper boundaries appropriate to a teacher's professional position • having regard for the need to safeguard pupils' well-being, in accordance with statutory provisions • showing tolerance of and respect for the rights of others • not undermining fundamental British values, including democracy, the rule of law, individual liberty and mutual respect, and tolerance of those with different faiths and beliefs • ensuring that personal beliefs are not expressed in ways which exploit pupils' vulnerability or might lead them to break the law. Teachers must have proper and professional regard for the ethos, policies and practices of the school in which they teach and maintain high standards in their own attendance and punctuality. Teachers must have an understanding of, and always act within, the statutory frameworks which set out their professional duties and responsibilities.

Discussion

Rather than focusing on what professionalism means to the teacher, we are going to look at our actions from the perspective of the child. First and foremost, children need to feel they can trust their teacher. Gillis and Nilsen (2017) conducted research to investigate how children reacted to adults saying a positive statement with negative body language and vice versa. They then compared it to how children responded to adults whose body language and statement matched. Children up to the age of five believed the verbal of statement of the adult, regardless of whether their facial expressions matched. By the age of six, the majority of children were untrusting of the adults whose bodies and words were at a discord. They found the children preferred the consistencies of those whose facial expressions backed up their words- even if the phrase and facial expression was negative (e.g. 'I have no stickers left'). They also commented that this work and that of Eskritt, Whalen and Lee (2008) suggest children are sensitive to violations of Gricean maxims.

Grice, a philosopher of languages, described conversation by the term 'co-operative principle', by which he meant contribute to the conversation in a rational and co-operative way. He expanded on this with four maxims as to what he felt co-operative conversation would be.

Maxim of Quantity: Information

- Make your contribution as informative as is required for the current purposes of the exchange.
- Don't make your contribution more informative than is required.

Maxim of Quality: Truth

- Do not say what you believe to be untrue.
- Do not say that for which you have insufficient evidence.

Maxim of Relation: Relevance

- Be relevant.

Maxim of Manner: Clarity

- Avoid obscurity of expression.
- Avoid ambiguity.
- Be brief (avoid unnecessary deviations).

(Grice, 1989)

The studies mentioned previously refer to children being sensitive to adults flouting these rules. To ensure children trust their teacher, they need to feel comfortable that maxims are not flouted in conversation with them, particularly the maxim of quality. It follows, then, that if we are going to be trusted so completely by the children in our class, then we must think carefully about what we say and what we convey through our actions on a day-to-day basis.

What is learned from school is much more than the statutory curriculum. If we imagine all that is learned at school as an iceberg, the national curriculum is just the visible tip. Underneath, there lies a hidden curriculum of norms, values and beliefs, and procedures – all absorbed by the children. The norms are more than the behavioural rules made explicit on walls and in policies; they are the conventions of the society of the school –examples would be the need to raise your hand to speak, or that some subjects are preferred by girls, or that children will be allowed to go home at the end of the day. The values and beliefs are linked to the view of education in this country – that learning is important and a right, that conforming is to be praised, it is good to be ambitious. The procedures – how and when to line up, wearing uniform and the behaviour rules are possibly the easiest of the three to articulate. Combined, they teach the children a considerable amount about what it means to be a part of a society.

Functional sociologists would say that the purpose of the hidden curriculum is to prepare young people for being a participant of society. Durkheim's view, as explained by Ottoway (1968) is that the norms and values teach a consensus and sense of solidarity which is vital to functioning in society. He also believed the meritocratic value of education taught the importance of having a good work ethic. Bowles and Gintis (1976) identify five ways that the hidden curriculum prepares for the workplace. They are that detentions and rules teach conformity and to follow rules whether or not it is what the individual desires; that boys and girls need to accept that they have different roles in society; to follow instructions from a superior; that punctuality is important and that respecting dominant ideas (like those taught in assemblies) is expected. Viewed through the lens of the 21st century, some of these ideas seem outdated compared to that which we would hold as values or beliefs in the modern day.

An alternative perspective on the purpose of the hidden curriculum is held by Liberalists such as Giroux and Penna (1979), who would argue that the hidden curriculum of norms and values is actually is constructed between pupils and adults, and as such can be constructed differently in each institution. If this is true, then there is tremendous potential for a school to carve a unique identity, bound together with a clearly defined culture of their own.

One such school is the Michaela free school in London. Their book, 'The Power of Culture', describes what it is that binds the school together and what they have chosen as their norms, values and beliefs. Their first book, 'Battle Hymn of the Tiger Teachers', gives clarity on the procedures they have constructed as part of this culture. Whether or not their view aligns with yours as to how a school should function, it is an incredible example of how norms, values, beliefs and procedures can coherently add up to a coherent culture. Another element that permeates through both books is that the teachers all 'buy in' to the culture – as reflected on in the traditionalist vs progressive debate, it is much easier to have 'proper and professional regard for the ethos, policies and practices of the school in which they teach'

(Teacher Standards, Part 2) when it aligns with your own views on education.

The introduction of British Values teaching (which was non-statutory but specifically sought out and commented upon in Ofsted inspections) by the DfE in 2014, is an interesting example of a topic that is threaded through both the visible and hidden curriculum. Values such as democracy, self-confidence and respect were no doubt part of almost every school's hidden curriculum long before the guidance was published. The change in 2014 was the transfer of these ideals to a more visible paradigm. Teachers were asked to specifically refer to these elements in other lessons, and to timetable opportunities to complete activities solely focusing on the teaching of these values. These lessons could be enacted from a functionalist or liberalist position, by explicitly teaching what it means to function in a democracy, from the responsibility to vote to the need to accept the rule of law. Alternatively, using a liberalist approach, negotiating what it means to be a citizen or issues around freedom to follow a particular faith could also be considered. This issue is not without controversy though. Maylor (2016) conducted research which demonstrated that teachers not only had different views on what British values actually were, but that they also had uninformed ideas regarding minority groups, which in some cases could even be considered racist. The recommendation was that initial teacher education needed to address this issue comprehensively. Alongside that, those currently teaching feel the need for more information than that given by completing PREVENT training. Without it, we are left with the negative statement of 'not undermining fundamental British values', rather than a more positive approach of actively encouraging them.

Learning Activities

Supporting Trainee Teachers

Talk to some children, this could be in your placement class, or from the School Council. Ask them what the school rules are; what is expected of them; if there is anything they just 'know' about how the school works. Do they feel uniform is important? Is there anything they would change about the culture of the school?

Supporting Newly Qualified Teachers

Visit www.booksfortopics.com - this is a great website for topic books on all areas of the curriculum as well as reading for pleasure. Select the booklists for 'Other topics' and look through the collections for Refugees and Immigrants, Politics and Democracy and British Values. Are there any copies of the books on the list in school for you to share with your class?

Supporting Early Career Teachers

Read 'Understanding British Values in Primary Schools' (Carroll et al, 2018) to gain insight into how to actively promote these elements in your practice.

Growing as a Mentor

Read 'Michaela: The Power of Culture' (ed. Birbalsingh, 2020) and consider the choices made about the culture in the school. If you were to design a school from the ground up, what would your culture be? What would you hope people would say as they walked round? What messages would the pupils infer about what you value?

Reflect on how black history is depicted in your school. Watch https://www.ted.com/talks/david_ikard_the_real_story_of_rosa_parks_and_why_we_need_to_confront_myths_about_black_history What hidden curriculum messages relating to race are evident – what else could be done?

References

Birbalsingh, K. ed. (2016) Battle Hymn of the Tiger Teachers, John Catt Educational, Woodbridge

Birbalsingh, K. ed. (2020) Michaela: The Power of Culture, John Catt Educational, Woodbridge

Caroll, J. Howard, C. Knight, B. (2018) Understanding British Values in Primary Schools- Policy and Practice, Learning Matters, Exeter

DfE (2014) Promoting Fundamental British Values as part of SMSC in schools, available at https://assets.publishing.service.gov.uk/government/uploads/system/uploads/attachment_data/file/380595/SMSC_Guidance_Maintained_Schools.pdf

Eskritt, M. Whalen, J. & Lee, K. (2008) *'Preschoolers can recognize violations of the Gricean maxims',* British Journal of Developmental Psychology. Oxford, UK: Blackwell Publishing Ltd, 26(3), pp435–443

Gillis, R. & Nilsen, E. (2017) *Consistency between verbal and non-verbal affective cues: a clue to speaker credibility*, Cognition and Emotion, 31(4), pp645-656

Giroux, H. & Penna, A. (1979) *Social Education in the Classroom: The Dynamics of the Hidden Curriculum. Theory and Research* in Social Education – Theory and research in social education 8(1), pp21-42

Grice, H. P. (1989). Studies in the way of words. Harvard University Press, Cambridge, MA

Ottaway, A. (1968) *Durkheim on Education,* British Journal of Educational Studies, *16*(1), pp5-16

Struthers, A. E. (2017) *'Teaching British Values in Our Schools',* Social & Legal Studies, SAGE Publications, London, 26(1), pp89–110

ACKNOWLEDGEMENTS

The Early Career Framework is reproduced under the open government licence for public sector information. A copy of this licence can be viewed here:
http://www.nationalarchives.gov.uk/doc/open-government-licence/version/3/

The Teachers' Standards are reproduced under the open government licence for public sector information. A copy of this licence can be viewed here:
http://www.nationalarchives.gov.uk/doc/open-government-licence/version/3/

ABOUT THE AUTHOR

Katie has been a primary school teacher since qualifying from King Alfred's College, Winchester, in 2003. Alongside teaching, she has completed post-graduate research in the use of CPA and textbooks in mathematics, improving reading comprehension and broadening vocabulary; and is currently completing a Master's degree in Education. Helping to develop an assessment system and foundation curriculum to meet the requirements of Curriculum 2014 whilst working as an Assistant Head, gave her a comprehensive understanding of the whole primary phase. Katie developed an interest in mentoring and supporting trainee and Newly Qualified Teachers whilst delivering PCP SCITT lectures in her role as an English subject lead. Since then, she has gone on to provide Art training for Fareham and Gosport SCITT trainees and written articles on classroom practice for Impact magazine. In her capacity as a Year Leader and Head of Key Stage, she has mentored trainees, NQTs and early career teachers- sometimes all at once!

contact: KatieJumpWrites@gmail.com

Printed in Great Britain
by Amazon

46656151R00063